Smarter Study Guides

How to succeed in Exams & Assessments

Kathleen McMillan and
Jonathan Weyers

PEARSON

Prentice
Hall

Harlow, England • London
Sydney • Tokyo • S
Cape Town • Madri

Pearson Education Limited
Edinburgh Gate
Harlow
Essex CM20 2JE
England

and Associated Companies throughout the world

Visit us on the World Wide Web at:
www.pearsoned.co.uk

First published 2007

ISBN: 978-0-273-71359-3

British Library Cataloguing-in-Publication Data
A catalogue record for this book is available from the British Library

10 9 8 7 6 5 4 3 2 1
10 09 08 07

Typeset in 9.5/13pt Interstate by 35
Printed and bound in Great Britain by Henry Ling Ltd, Dorchester, Dorset

The Publisher's policy is to use paper manufactured from sustainable forests.

Smarter Study Guides

Instant answers to your most pressing university skills problems.

Are there any secrets to successful study?

The simple answer is no – but there are some essential skills, tips and techniques that can help you to improve your performance and success in all areas of your university studies.

These handy, easy-to-use guides to the most common areas where most students need help (even if you don't realise it!) provide accessible, straightforward practical tips and instant solutions that provide you with the tools and techniques that will enable you to improve your performance and get better results – and better grades!

Each book in the series allows you to assess and address a particular set of skills and strategies, in crucial areas such as exam preparation and performance, researching and writing dissertations and research projects and planning and crafting academic essays. Each book then delivers practical no-nonsense tips, techniques and strategies that will enable you to significantly improve your abilities and performance in time to make a difference.

The books in the series are

- *How to succeed in Exams and Assessments*
- *How to write Essays and Assignments*
- *How to write Dissertations and Project Reports*

Or for a complete handbook covering all of the study skills that you will need throughout your years at university:

- *The Smarter Student: Study Skills and Strategies for Success at University*

Get smart, get a head start!

The Smarter Student series is available at all good bookshops or online at **www.pearson-books.co.uk/studyskills**

Contents

Stress management

As the exam approaches

Tackling specific types of exam and assessment

Preface and acknowledgements

Welcome to *How to Succeed in Exams and Assessments*. We're pleased you have chosen this book and hope it will fulfil its promise and help you achieve excellent grades. Our aim has been to provide tried-and-tested tips covering the whole exam experience, from planning your revision to coping with exam nerves. We've tried to remain faithful to the philosophy of our earlier book, *The Smarter Student*, by creating a quickly accessible resource that you can dip into in time of need. We had many kinds of students in mind when we decided to write this text and we hope that it will meet your personal needs – regardless of your experience and background.

We would like to offer sincere thanks to many people who have influenced us and contributed to the development and production of this book. Countless people over the years have helped us to test our ideas, especially our PREP resit summer school tutors and students, who provided valuable feedback. We are grateful to the following colleagues and collaborators who have helped us directly or indirectly: Margaret Adamson, Michael Allardice, Chris Carter, Kate Christie, Anne-Marie Greenhill, Jane Illés, Jane Prior, Anne Scott, David Walker, Amanda Whitehead, Will Whitfield and Hilary-Kay Young. Also, we acknowledge those at other universities who have helped frame our thoughts, particularly our good friends Rob Reed, Nicki Hedge and Esther Daborn. We owe a special debt to the senior colleagues who encouraged various projects that contributed to this book, and who allowed us the freedom to pursue this avenue of scholarship, especially Robin Adamson, Ian Francis, Rod Herbert and David Swinfen. At Pearson Education, we have had excellent advice and support from Steve Temblett, Georgina Clark-Mazo and Joan Dale Lace. Finally, we would like to say thanks to our long-suffering but nevertheless enthusiastic families: Derek, Keith and Fiona; and Mary, Paul and James, all of whom helped in various capacities.

We'd be delighted to hear your opinion of the book and receive any suggestions you have for additions and improvements.

Kathleen McMillan and Jonathan Weyers
University of Dundee
April 2007

How to use this book

How to Succeed in Exams and Assessments has been organised and designed to be as user-friendly as possible. Each chapter is self-contained and deals with a particular aspect of learning, revision or assessment/exam technique. You can therefore read the book through from end-to-end, or in sections, or dip into specific chapters as and when you think you need them.

At the start of each chapter you'll find a brief paragraph and a **Key topics** list, which lets you know what's included. There is also a list of *Key terms* at this point, and, should you be uncertain about the meaning of any of these, you'll find definitions in the Glossary (pp. 187–91).

Within each chapter, the text is laid out to help you absorb the key concepts easily, using headings and bulleted lists to help you find what you need as efficiently as possible. Relevant examples are contained in figures, tables and boxes, which can be consulted independently, if necessary. The inset boxes are of three types:

 Smart tip boxes emphasise key advice to ensure you adopt a successful approach.

 Information boxes provide additional information, such as useful definitions or examples.

 Query boxes raise questions for you to consider about your personal approach to the topic.

 At the end of each chapter, there's a **Practical tips** section with additional tips. You should regard this as a menu from which to select the ideas that appeal to you and your learning personality.

 Finally, the **And now** box provides three suggestions that you could consider as ideas to take further.

→ Introduction

Succeeding in exams and assessments

Understanding the processes involved in revision and exam-sitting

This book aims to support students who want to succeed in university exams. Achieving this goal will be much easier if you start with a mental picture of the different processes involved in revision and exam-sitting and use this information to arrive at a strategy to guide your efforts.

Key topics:

→ Information gathering
→ Information processing
→ Information retrieval and delivery

Key terms
Autonomous learner   Learning objectives   Learning outcomes
Learning styles   Marking criteria

If you wish to revise effectively, it is crucial that you know what you are trying to accomplish. One way of gaining this understanding is to divide the revision and exam-sitting process into components and look at what you need to achieve at each stage. The process is essentially about managing information – the facts and understanding gained during your course – and can be separated into three main elements:

● information gathering;
● information processing; and
● information retrieval and delivery.

If you do the right things in each of these phases you will greatly increase your chances of achieving excellent grades.

As a result of attending lectures, tutorials or practicals, and from carrying out additional background reading, you will have access to a large amount of information in the form of lecture notes, handouts, printouts (for example, PowerPoint presentations), tutorial or practical notes, textbooks, notes from textbooks and other sources, coursework you may have carried out, and online material. You will probably be able to consult two other vital resources: learning objectives (or learning outcomes) and past exam papers. You should not forget to consult any feedback that you received on coursework assignments as this may give you useful direction on areas of weakness or aspects that require more attention on your part.

In this phase of revision your aim is to ensure that you have copies of all that you require close to hand, and to make sure that it is well organised so that you can consult what you need, quickly:

❑ Check that you have all the lecture notes and make arrangements to download or copy them, if you do not have these things in place.
❑ File your notes in sequence.
❑ Buy or borrow the textbooks that support your course (check the reading list in the course handbook). Alternatively, look these up in your library catalogue and place reservations on them if they are available only on limited access.
❑ Gather together all other materials that might be relevant, such as completed coursework with feedback.
❑ Bookmark any online resources that you might be expected to consult.
❑ Obtain copies of past papers and model answers, if available.
❑ Find out where the learning objectives or outcomes are published (for example in the course handbook), and make a copy of them.
❑ Look in your course handbook for any special guidance notes on the exam and its format.

---

smart tip

Managing the time taken for information gathering

You must not let the information gathering phase take up too much of your revision time – recognise that it can be a displacement activity and limit the time you allocate to it within your revision timetable (Ch 8).

There are many potential sources of information about any topic, and a key aspect of your early university education is that you are guided by your tutors as to what is important and reliable, and what is not. Students at higher levels are expected to carry out elements of this task for themselves, as autonomous learners. Working out exactly how much and what kind of extra information you require is closely linked to how you will need to process it.

What is autonomous learning?

At university, you are normally expected to frame your own learning within the context of your course. This self-management is often referred to as 'autonomy' and means that you need to be able to work on your own, defining the knowledge and understanding that you need to achieve goals, solve problems and create new outcomes. The ability to learn autonomously develops over time. As you become more experienced as a student, you will recognise and develop skills and approaches that will make you an independent learner.

→ Information processing

This revision phase involves analysing and manipulating the material you have gathered, with the learning objectives and past exam papers in mind. The principle is not to study passively, for example, by reading through the written material, but to try to do something active, to help you to memorise it (**Ch 11** and **Ch 12**).

Thinking about thinking

It is important to recognise that university teaching is not solely about information transfer where you just accumulate information and memorise a series of facts from lectures and other source material. You must be able *use* information. In short, you must develop skills in critical thinking. The facts are still required, but it is what you do with them in response to the exam or assessment instruction that is important (**Ch 15**). Benjamin Bloom, a noted educational psychologist, and colleagues, identified six different stages involved in the acquisition of learning and the process of thinking. These are popularly listed as:

- Knowledge
- Comprehension
- Application
- Analysis
- Synthesis
- Evaluation

Bloom *et al.* (1956) showed that students were expected to progress through this scale of thought-processing during their studies (Table 1.1). Looking at this table, you may recognise that your school work mainly focussed on knowledge, comprehension and application, while your university tutors tend to expect more in terms of analysis, synthesis and evaluation. These expectations are sometimes closely linked to the instruction words used in exam questions. Table 1.1 provides a few examples. However, take care when interpreting these instructions, as processes and tasks may mean different things in different subjects. For example, while 'description' might imply a

Table 1.1 A classification of learning objectives derived from the work of Benjamin Bloom and colleagues

Taxonomy of learning objectives (in ascending order of difficulty)	Typical question instructions
Knowledge. If you know a fact, you have it at your disposal and can *recall* or *recognise* it. This does not mean you necessarily understand it at a higher level	• Define • Describe • Identify
Comprehension. To comprehend a fact means that you *understand* what it means	• Contrast • Discuss • Interpret
Application. To apply a fact means that you can *put it to use*	• Demonstrate • Calculate • Illustrate
Analysis. To analyse information means that you are able to *break it down into parts* and show how these components *fit together*	• Analyse • Explain • Compare
Synthesis. To synthesise, you need to be able to *extract relevant facts* from a body of knowledge and use these to *address an issue in a novel way* or *create something new*	• Compose • Create • Integrate
Evaluation. If you evaluate information, you *arrive at a judgement* based on its importance relative to the topic being addressed	• Recommend • Support • Draw a conclusion

lower-level activity in the arts, it might involve high-level skills in subjects such as architecture.

When you analyse the instructions used in exam questions, you should take into account what type of thinking process the examiner has asked you to carry out, and try your best to reach the required level.

Thinking about learning

On coming to university, it may be useful to consider or reconsider the ways in which you learn best. This is a personal matter: people differ greatly in their preferences for processing and retrieving information. For some students, developing an understanding of this aspect of their character makes a huge difference to their levels of attainment. In **Ch 4** we discuss various types of learning personality, different methods of diagnosing your learning style, and the best ways of approaching study and revision once you know where your learning preferences lie.

Understanding the university exam system

Your department or school will provide plenty of helpful information about assessment. You can find it in course or programme handbooks, printed or online. Accessing this material will help you process the course material and your notes appropriately.

● **Learning objectives/outcomes.** These signify what your tutors believe you should be able to accomplish after participating in the different parts of the syllabus and carrying out the further studies they have recommended. They are a vital resource to you when revising, as they will help you interpret the course materials correctly and gain clues about the sorts of exam questions that will be set (see **Ch 9**).

---

smart tip

Keys to successful information processing

As part of an approach based on active revision, you will probably wish to reduce or 'distil' the notes you have made (**Ch 11**). This can only be done effectively with a clear idea of the sorts of question that will be asked and an indication of the depth at which you will be expected to deal with the material. In part, this information can be obtained by studying the learning objectives or outcomes and past exam papers.

- **Design of exam papers.** To process information effectively as part of your revision, it is essential to look at past papers. These will be valuable in three respects:

  - **Type of exam.** Tutors use different forms of assessment, depending on which aspects of your learning that they wish to observe (**Ch 17** and **Ch 21**). If you understand why they have chosen a particular form, you can adjust your revision strategy to take this into account.

  - **Style of questions.** The ways in which you will be expected to process the information you have collated can be deduced from the style of questions in past papers. For example, you can figure out the scope of knowledge and depth of understanding that will be expected by relating each question to the learning objectives and the syllabus as taught (**Ch 9**).

  - **Weighting of marks.** Information about the proportion of marks allocated to different questions or sections of a paper will give you an indication of the effort you should put into each topic within your revision timetable (and during the exam). As a rough guide, the proportion of time spent revising, or answering specific questions in exams, should match the proportion of marks allocated. However, you may wish to adjust this balance if a particular topic is difficult for you (**Ch 8** and **Ch 15**).

If past papers are not available in any of your subjects, you should consider meeting with others in your class to see if, together, you can come up with ideas about potential questions and styles of question (**Ch 6** and **Ch 9**).

---

smart tip

Beware of changes to the syllabus or to the construction of exam papers

It is worth remembering that courses may change over time, as can the staff teaching them. This can have a considerable impact on content and the course structure. These should be flagged to you within the course handbook, or by tutors, but it might be worth confirming with the course leader or departmental administrator if you see a mismatch between the syllabus as taught and the learning objectives or question papers. The same applies to checking whether you can assume that this year's exam papers will be constructed in the same way as in previous years.

- **Marking criteria.** These statements indicate the levels of attainment that tutors expect for different grades (**Ch 2**). They are the benchmarks for assessing the evidence of your learning, as shown in your responses to assessments and exams. The marking criteria are useful to look at before you start revising: allied with an understanding of Table 1.1, they will give you a better feel for how deep your understanding should be and for the standards that apply to your work.

---

smart tip

Using feedback from past exams and assessment

Feedback you have received about your previous exam and assessment performances (**Ch 10**) should affect how you carry out information processing during revision. For example, this might indicate that your answers have lacked relevance or sufficient depth. You should therefore adjust your approach to reflect any comments, perhaps by ensuring that you are applying higher-level thinking skills (Table 1.1) or have committed relevant facts to memory (**Ch 12**).

→ Information retrieval and delivery

The important part of this phase will occur within the exam hall as you answer the specific questions that have been set, but it is vital to recognise that you can practise the skills involved. By doing so, you can reduce nerves and enter the exam hall with confidence. Ways of doing this are discussed throughout this book, and include:

- Refining the techniques you employ for memorising (**Ch 11** and **Ch 12**).
- Testing yourself on individual elements you feel you need to know (**Ch 12**).
- Practising answering exam questions in mock exams (**Ch 9**).
- Discussing how you would approach exams and potential exam questions with a 'study buddy' (**Ch 6**).
- In quantitative subjects, practising numerical problems (**Ch 18**).

Having an exam strategy (**Ch 15**) is essential to ensure that you balance your efforts when 'delivering' information in your answers.

Practical tips for making the most of your revision time

Create a revision timetable. The two most important things you can do to make the most of your revision time are to create a plan for your work quickly and to stick to it in a disciplined way (**Ch 7** and **Ch 8**). Without this underpinning, all the other tips given in this book will be reduced in their effectiveness. Remember that you do not need to make your timetable into a work of art as there is always a danger that this becomes a displacement activity that prevents you getting down to real work – a common but flawed strategy that achieves a lot on paper but not much in terms of learning.

Map out the gathering, processing and retrieval aspects of revision within your revision timetable. You should set aside time for each activity.

- Information gathering must occur at the start (or should already have been accomplished), but should not take too long.
- Information processing will probably be the longest phase, and it is worth punctuating it with sessions where you deliberately cross-reference your efforts to learning objectives and past exam papers.
- It is important to set aside some time close to the exams for practising your information retrieval skills.

Spend some time reflecting on past exam performances. Think about changes that you could make to your revision approach that might improve your future performance.

Sort out your non-academic life. You will need space and time to revise properly. Adjust your social commitments as appropriate; ask friends and family to help you out temporarily, perhaps with shopping, cooking or washing. Tidy up your working space so you can study in an organised way.

1.1 Find out where learning objectives and past papers are located. Obtain copies at an early stage, and read them as the course material is presented, making notes about how you might wish to adjust your revision strategy to take account of them. For example, you might feel you will need to delve more deeply into certain areas, making extra notes. Alternatively, you might see that there is an expectation for you to read about a specific topic by yourself.

1.2 Create a suitable filing system. If you can develop this as your course proceeds, rather than during your revision time, you will be able to spend less time organising your notes prior to the information processing stage, and will therefore be able to spend as much time as possible understanding and learning the material.

1.3 Take the time to look into your learning personality. Consult **Ch 4** for further information. If you already have a good feel for what your learning personality is, then consider what changes to your previous revision approach you could make to take account of this.

What markers are looking for

Assessment at university

How tests and examinations work

University assessment systems are complex and rather different from those used at school or college. This chapter clarifies the terminology involved and explains the rationale for different modes of assessment, while later chapters discuss how to tackle specific question types.

Key topics:

→ Forms of assessment
→ Marking criteria and grading schemes
→ Modules and progression
→ Degree classifications and transcripts

Key terms
Aggregate mark   Class exam   Exam diet   External examiner   Finals
Formative assessment   Learning objective   Marking criteria
Oral exam   Peer assessment   Summative assessment   Transcript

A university is an educational institution with a legal charter entitling it to award its own degrees. These degrees are granted on the basis of performance in assessments and exams, which may vary in character depending on subject and institution. As a result, each university has its own conventions regarding style of question, format of exams and marking criteria. No two universities are the same. It is essential that you take into account how the exam system operates in your own institution *before* you start revising.

smart tip

Exam format

This should never come as a surprise to you as you should have checked up on it by looking at past papers and by confirming with lecturers that there have been no changes to the style of examination.

Exam papers and diets may be structured in different ways, according to discipline. The design may reflect the different aspects of learning that your tutors wish to assess (Ch 17 and Ch 19). For example, there may be a multiple-choice component that tests your surface knowledge across a wide range of topics, while an essay section may be included to test your deeper knowledge in fewer topics. Papers and questions may carry different weightings towards an aggregate mark.

Various levels of choice are given to reflect the nature of the field of study. In professional disciplines there may be a need to ensure you are knowledgeable in all areas, while in other subjects a certain amount of specialisation may be acceptable. Some exam papers are divided into sections, and you will be expected to answer one or more questions from the options within each of these. This format allows a limited amount of choice while ensuring that you have covered all major areas in your studies. It is vital that you take these aspects of exam paper design into account when arriving at a strategy for revision and exam-sitting (Ch 15).

→ Forms of assessment

Each degree programme and every unit of teaching at university (usually called a 'module') will have a published set of aims and learning objectives or outcomes. Your performance in relation to these goals will be tested in various ways.

- **Formative assessments** are primarily designed to give you feedback on the quality of your answers. In some cases these are known as 'class exams'. They generally do not count towards your final module assessment, although sometimes a small proportion of marks will carry forward as an incentive to perform well.

- **Summative assessments** count directly towards a module or degree assessment. Many summative exams are held as formal invigilated tests where you work in isolation. These may be known as degree exams and, in the honours year, in some institutions, as 'finals'. These exams may comprise several sittings or papers, perhaps covering different aspects of the course, and often lasting for two or three hours each. The collective set of exams is sometimes known as an exam diet.

In some cases, in-course work will count towards degree exams (continuous assessment). This can take the form of essays, projects, and special exercises like problem-based learning. However, the majority of marks are usually devoted to formal invigilated exams where the possibility of collaboration, plagiarism and impersonation are limited, and you will be expected to perform alone under a certain amount of time pressure.

Problem-based learning (PBL)

This is a form of learning where you are asked to investigate a specific problem, usually related to a real-life professional situation, which may be open-ended in nature (that is, not necessarily having a 'right answer'). You may be part of a small team asked to consider the problem, research the underlying theory and practice that might lead to a response, and arrive at a practical solution. Assessment of the exercise will focus not only on the solution you arrive at, but also on the way in which you arrive at it, so here process is often at least as important as the product. There may be group- and peer-assessment elements to your grade.

→ Marking criteria and grading schemes

Who marks your papers? How do they do it? Often students are unsure about this. The norm is for papers to be graded by the person who delivered the lectures, tutorials or practical classes. With large classes, alternative mechanisms may be employed:

- the marking may be spread out among several tutors;
- especially in multiple-choice papers, the marking may be automated;
- where teamwork is involved, peer assessment may take place.

Peer assessment

This is where the members of a study team are asked to assign a mark to each other's performance. This might take account, for example, of the effort put in, the conduct in the assigned team role(s), and contribution to the final outcome. Clear guidance is always given about how you should assign marks.

Each university will publish assessment reporting scales, usually in handbooks and/or websites. Some operate to a familiar system of banded percentages, often related to honours degree classifications, while others adopt a different form of band 'descriptors'. Find out which system applies in your case and consult the general marking criteria used to assign work in each band. This will give you a better idea of the standard of work needed to produce a specific grade, and may help you to understand feedback.

To maintain standards and ensure fairness, several systems operate:

- There may be an explicit marking scheme that allocates a proportion of the total to different aspects of your answer.
- Double- or triple-marking may take place and if the grades awarded differ, then the answer may be scrutinised more closely, possibly by a external examiner.
- Papers are usually marked anonymously, so the marker does not know whose answer they are grading.
- The external marker will confirm the overall standard and may inspect some papers, particularly those falling at the division between honours grades or on the pass/fail boundary.
- Accreditation bodies in the professions may be involved in the examination process, and some answer papers may be marked by external assessors appointed by these accrediting bodies rather than by university staff.

External examiners

These are appointed by the university to ensure standards are maintained and that the assessment is fair. They are usually noted academics in the field, with wide experience of examining. They review the exam question papers in advance and will generally look closely at a representative selection of written papers and project work. For finals, they may interview students in an oral, to ensure that spoken responses meet the standard of the written answers, and to arrive at a judgement on borderline cases.

Modular systems of study at university have been developed for several reasons:

- they allow greater flexibility in subject choice;
- they can efficiently accommodate students studying different degree paths;
- they make it easier for students to transfer between courses and institutions;
- they break up studies into 'bite-sized' elements and allow exams to be spread out more evenly over the academic year.

The set of modules that make up a degree programme are carefully selected to build on each other in a complementary way, and to allow you to develop skills that you can take forward to the next level of study. Therefore, you should avoid:

- dodging seemingly difficult or unattractive subjects;
- 'closing the book' on a subject once it has been assessed; or
- limiting your degree options.

Modules are usually assessed in a summative end-of-module exam, perhaps with a component from in-course assessment. In some subjects, borderline cases are given an extra oral exam. If you fail the end-of-module exam (and any oral), a resit is normally possible. Resits usually take place towards the end of the summer vacation. The result is usually based solely on your performance in the resit exam.

At the end of each academic year, and after any resits, you will be required to fulfil certain progression criteria that allow you to pass on to the next level of study. These criteria are normally published in course handbooks. If you fail to satisfy the criteria, you may need to resit the whole year or even to leave the university. Sometimes you may be asked to 'carry' specific modules: that is, study them again in addition to the normal quota for your next year of study. Some institutions may place a condition on your re-entry, for example, achieving a certain level of marks or passing a prescribed number of modules in order to progress. This would normally be discussed with your adviser/director of studies.

Appeals against termination of studies

Your studies may be terminated for one of several reasons but most commonly failure to meet attendance or progression criteria. Occasionally, termination will be enforced due to disciplinary reasons, for example, in a case of plagiarism. Students will normally be offered a chance to appeal and will be expected to produce evidence of any extenuating circumstances, such as medical certificates, or notes from support service personnel. Such students may also wish to ask tutors to support their application where the tutor is aware of their personal situation.

→ Degree classifications and transcripts

Students with superior entry qualifications or experience may join university at different levels. There are also a range of exit awards – certificates, diplomas and ordinary degrees. However, the majority of students now enter at level 1, and study for an honours degree. This encompasses three years of study in England, Wales and Northern Ireland, and four years in Scotland. Credit will normally be given for years of study carried out abroad or in work placement, according to specific schemes operated by your university. This includes participation in European Community schemes such as ERASMUS or LINGUA (see **http://europa.eu.int/index_en.htm**).

Sometimes entry into the final honours year is competitive, based on grades in earlier years. Some universities operate a junior honours year, which means you are accepted into an honours stream at an earlier stage and may have special module options.

Nearly all universities follow the same honours degrees grading system, which are, in descending order:

- first class (a 'first')
- upper second class (a two-one or 2:1)
- lower second class (a two-two or 2:2)
- third class (a 'third')
- unclassified.

(Universities may not differentiate between the second-class divisions.)

In some institutions, these classifications will take into account all grades you have obtained during your university career; sometimes only those in junior and senior honours years; and in the majority, only grades obtained in the finals. This makes the finals critical, especially as there are no resits for them.

Once your degree classification has been decided by the examination committee or board, and moderated by the external examiner, it will be passed for ratification to the university's senate or equivalent body for academic legislation. During this period you will technically be a graduand, until your degree is conferred at the graduation ceremony. At this time you will receive a diploma certificate and be entitled to wear a colourful degree- and institution-specific 'hood' for your gown.

Job prospects with different degrees

In a competitive job market, your chances of being considered for a position may depend on your degree classification, but employers also take into account other personal qualities and experience. Research positions that involve reading for a higher degree, such as an MSc or PhD, usually require a first or 2:1.

Employers will usually ask to see your diploma for confirmation of your degree and may contact the university to confirm your qualification and obtain a copy of your transcript. This document shows your performance in *all* assessments throughout your career at the university.

Practical tips for understanding the assessment system

Ask senior students about the exam system. They may have useful tips and advice to pass on.

Find out where essential information is recorded. This could be in a combination of handbooks and web-based resources.

If you don't understand any aspect of the assessment system, ask course administrators or tutors. Knowing how the system works is important and can affect your performance.

Notify your institution of any disability

If you have a disability, you should make the institution aware of this. You may have special concessions in exams, for example, using the services of a scribe, being allowed extra time, or having exam question papers printed in large print for you. Appropriate entitlements take time to arrange and you must ensure that arrangements are in place well before the exam date. Contact your department and disability support service for guidance.

(GO) And now . . .

2.1 Carry out the necessary research to ensure you know how your university's exam system works for your intended degree. You should find out about:

- course and degree programme aims
- learning objectives or outcomes
- the format of assessments and proportion of in-course and final exam elements
- timing of exam diets
- assessment or marking criteria
- the grading scheme
- weighting of exam components
- progression criteria

2.2 Find out about in-course assessments and how they will contribute to your module or degree grade. Your course handbooks will normally include this information. Marks for in-course work can often be influenced by the amount of work you put in, so they can be a good way of ensuring you create a strong platform to perform well in summative exams.

2.3 Examine past exam papers in your subjects to investigate how they are constructed. This will allow you to see whether there are subdivisions, restrictions or other features that might influence your revision or exam strategies.

Physical and mental preparation

3 | Physical and mental preparation

How to gear up for assessment and exam-sitting

To achieve your full potential in assessments and exams, your brain needs to be operating at its best. This also means that the rest of your body will need to be in good physical condition, as the health of body and mind are linked closely. This chapter explains how you can ensure that you are in the best possible shape in the run-up to exams.

Key topics:
→ Well-being, health and nutrition
→ The role of physical exercise
→ Mental exercise, relaxation and sleep
→ Thinking positively

Key terms
Caffeine   Micronutrients   Vitamins

Good academic performance depends on your mind operating at or near to its peak ability, but we're all aware that our intellectual powers vary according to a range of influences, and are not always at their best. Having a better understanding of factors that influence your brain's function will help you prepare better for your forthcoming assessments or exams.

→ Well-being, health and nutrition

Most experts agree that that a healthy mind thrives in a healthy body. However, we don't always take care of our bodies or minds in the best possible way. For students, this condition may result from any of a number of factors related to university life. If you wish to take a professional approach to your exams, you may need to look for ways in which you can adapt your lifestyle to ensure that you are in the best possible physical and mental shape to face your exams. Table 3.1 provides a checklist of things to do, and things not to do, as you approach your exams. You may wish to focus on some of the following:

- **Regulating your sleep pattern.** Try to ensure that you have enough sleep and make sure that your pattern of waking coincides with the general working day, and in particular with your exam times.

- **Avoiding or cutting down chemical influences likely to interfere with your mental capacity.** The chief of these is likely to be alcohol, a known depressant. Others include nicotine, certain prescription drugs and most non-prescription drugs.

- **Avoiding overuse of stimulants.** Taking chemicals like caffeine (present in tea, coffee, 'Red Bull' and Coke-like drinks) may provide a temporary boost, but there is an inevitable downside after this, and your sleep pattern may be disrupted.

- **Keeping well hydrated.** Your water intake or lack of it has known effects on the ability to concentrate and learn.

- **Knowing how and when to relax.** Exercise has an important role to play here, as does escapism, such as watching a film or playing games. Near to exams, these leisure and rest activities should not take up too much time, but they should remain a part of your timetable.

Table 3.1 **A quick checklist of things to do and things not to do to improve your preparation for exams**

Positives (try to do these)	Negatives (try not to do these)
❏ Gain mental agility (puzzles, quizzes, sums, examples, reading)	❏ Abuse alcohol or other drugs that may impair your mental capacity
❏ Improve mental stamina (work for longer periods)	❏ Be distracted by less important things (e.g. TV programmes, socialising)
❏ Become fitter (a healthy mind in a healthy body)	❏ Study so much you do not sleep enough or distort your waking rhythm
❏ Eat well	❏ Avoid key topics that you dislike
❏ Get your body clock in tune with 'exam time'	❏ Read your notes rather than carry out appropriate active revision methods
❏ Clean away clutter and start with a clear desk	❏ Carry out unfocussed revision that fails to take account of learning objectives
❏ Sleep well (make sure you are physically as well as mentally tired)	
❏ Carry out active revision that takes account of your learning style	

You should try to eat well when studying as your brain requires a good supply of energy and essential nutrients. A good breakfast is a good idea to kick-start your day, followed by light snacks to keep your energy levels up. Small, frequent snacks are best because after you eat large meals there are known hormonal responses that slow down metabolism and mental activity, leading to drowsiness and lethargy. If this effect is familiar to you, avoid fatty foods and note that more complex carbohydrates like starch provide a more slowly released supply of sugars.

Vitamins and micronutrients are known to enhance health and mental activity. Anyone who eats healthily should not be deficient in these dietary factors, but you may wish to consult a health professional if in doubt over the use of vitamin supplements.

If you feel unwell in the period prior to exams, you should visit your doctor or university health service, not only in hope of a diagnosis and treatment, but also to obtain necessary documentation that might explain a weak performance.

Vitamins and micronutrients and what they do

Vitamin A: antioxidant. Important for vision; enhances immunity and helps prevent infections such as colds.

Vitamin B complex (there are at least twelve B vitamins): primary effects as enzyme cofactors, so important in ensuring that metabolism functions smoothly; also important for blood turnover. Many known effects on mental well-being. Certain B vitamins may need to be supplemented in athletes, alcohol drinkers and those taking the female oral contraceptive.

Vitamin C: antioxidant; important in fat metabolism and may boost immune system. Levels may be lowered by alcohol, painkillers or nicotine. Deficiency can result in depression.

Vitamin D: important in nutrient absorption and growth; beneficial effects on the immune system.

Vitamin E: antioxidant; important for blood function and circulation.

Micronutrients: most act as enzyme cofactors. Iron is essential for healthy blood function. Lack of magnesium and zinc have known effects on mental health.

(Sources: Rutherford, 2002; Graham, 2006)

→ The role of physical exercise

Aerobic exercise is an excellent way to relax mentally, reduce stress and improve sleep patterns. Carried out regularly over a long period, exercise improves your stamina, a valuable commodity for extended exam schedules, which can be physically exhausting as well as mentally draining. Non-aerobic and meditation workouts such as yoga, Pilates and Tai Chi also have potential to help you in the run-up to exams by helping you to relax.

Exercise is also important in the short term because it stimulates brain activity by improving the blood supply to your brain, an organ that requires a surprising amount of oxygen and energy to function well. You should try to do some physical activity, even if it is as simple as a walk or swim, on most revision days. This basic exercise is probably the best quick fix to remove feelings of mental lethargy.

→ Mental exercise, relaxation and sleep

As an organ, your brain responds to being exercised. In a similar fashion to your muscles, the more it works, the better prepared it is for future effort. Unsurprisingly, revision itself is an excellent mental preparation for exams. This 'exercise' factor is independent from memorisation carried out during your revision; as you move through your revision timetable, your brain will become used to its daily mental workout and will be better prepared for the challenge of the exams.

Key facts about your brain

Your brain takes up only about 2 per cent of your body's mass, yet it receives some 15 per cent of your blood circulation. It consumes about a fifth of your total oxygen intake, and metabolises roughly a quarter of your body's glucose. Your brain absorbs approximately 50 per cent of the oxygen and 10 per cent of glucose circulating in your arterial bloodstream.

(Source: Magistretti et al., 2000)

Some ideas for exercising and relaxing your mind

Exercise:

- ❏ doing puzzles like crosswords and sudoku
- ❏ playing computer games (not in excess)
- ❏ taking part in TV and pub quizzes
- ❏ reading for leisure (in short bursts)

Relaxing:

- ❏ shutting your eyes and breathing slowly and deeply for 2-3 minutes
- ❏ watching films or TV soap operas
- ❏ taking a brief walk or swim
- ❏ having a bath, jacuzzi or sauna

These activities should be brief, relaxing and should not impinge on timetabled periods of study. Ideally, they should be incorporated into your revision timetable (Ch 8).

Equally, there will be times when your mind needs to relax. This can be accomplished by focussing your thoughts on a completely different matter. Physical activities and games can have this useful effect. A good sleep pattern is vital to rest your brain between intensive study sessions and before exams. Unfortunately, the anxiety many people feel immediately prior to exams is not conducive to sleep. If you have this as a persistent problem, you may wish to adopt some of the following tips, suggested by McKenna (2006):

- Get up earlier, consistently – this has the effect of making you more tired at the end of the day.
- Keep a consistent waking routine (even at weekends) – you can control this element, but not when you feel tired.
- Go to bed only when you feel ready to sleep.
- Keep bed for sleep – if you want to read, watch TV or eat, then relax in a living space to do this.
- If you generally feel that afternoons are not your best time for studying, then exercising in the afternoon can be helpful as a way of freshening you up for a study stint when you are more alert later in the day.

- Eat and drink (especially stimulants like caffeine and depressants like alcohol) well ahead of the time that you plan to go to bed.
- Rather than toss and turn when you cannot sleep, get up and do something useful until you feel tired.
- Drift off to sleep thinking about positives, rather than negatives.
- Tell yourself a story, preferably a boring one, as you attempt to fall asleep.

Maintaining a regular and appropriate sleep pattern smart tip

Your aim should be to align your waking times to the times of your exams. Some people like to rise early and others to rise late. Some people find that napping during the day is helpful as a means of giving them a second wind, while others find that this puts them off regular sleep patterns. Whichever type you are, remember that exams mostly fit into the working day and you must make sure that your regime has not turned night into day.

→ Thinking positively

A key aspect of mental preparation for exams is to think positively. When you start to revise and are confronted by all your reading material, notes and seemingly endless facts and concepts, it is easy to become despondent and feel that there is too much to do in the time available. These sorts of thoughts can result in a negative spiral where you put off effective work and never actually get going.

These tips will help you adopt a positive frame of mind when revising:

- Get started on your studies, somehow. Don't put off this crucial moment. Once you become engaged with the material, your natural curiosity and interest in the subject will take over. Even if the topics have not seemed interesting in the past, once you begin to understand them in depth, they may become more so.
- Adopt an approach of breaking large topics into smaller chunks. That way each time you complete a section you will feel you have made progress.
- Make sure you mark off what you have completed in your revision timetable (**Ch 8**) as you cover the material. After a few sessions,

this visual summary should give you a feeling of having made real inroads into the task.

- Link up with someone else studying the same subject and make a pact to try to encourage each other (Ch 6). Quizzing each other or working together on areas of the course that you both find difficult can help both parties feel more in control of the subject matter and, if you continue to have difficulty, then you can go together to speak with your lecturer or tutor about your queries.

- Focus on the main goal (your degree, and the type of job you hope will come after it) and reflect on how each small study session is one small step on this important journey in your life.

- Recall positive experiences from your past exam-sitting history, focussing on how your hard work paid dividends in the end, despite any lack of confidence you may have felt at the time.

In the vital period just before you enter the exam hall, it is important to be completely focussed and positive. Although there are benefits from meeting up with fellow students and sharing feelings and ideas about potential exam questions, these exchanges will almost certainly make you more nervous. If this is likely to be the case, find a spot nearby where you can gather your thoughts in peace and then time your entry to the exam hall to avoid meeting your friends. Things to concentrate on during this period are:

- your exam strategy – how you plan to tackle this particular paper (Ch 15);

- your approach to the questions – how you plan to structure your answers;

- key facts or formulae (you are unlikely to memorise them at this stage, but running over them may keep them fresh in your mind if you have already learnt them by heart: Ch 12);

- what you plan to do when all your exams are finished and how quickly this particular exam will be over;

- your determination to succeed and how you aim to squeeze every mark possible out of your brain in response to the instructions on the exam paper;

- how you plan to ensure your answers are relevant; and

- how you need to be working quickly and effectively for every second of the exam.

Practical tips to help prepare yourself for exams

Ensure you eat healthily. This should include eating the right amount of calories (neither too many, nor too few) and plenty of fruit and vegetables.

Give 'you' some time. Studying without any let-up won't necessarily mean that you will do more. Taking some time out for you – listening to music, reading a novel, playing a game, pampering yourself with a favourite activity – will make you feel good about yourself and contribute to your sense of confidence and well-being. It will also help create a sense of revitalised motivation.

Go for a short walk. If you are feeling drowsy or lacking in concentration or focus when revising, go outside for a quick walk. A brisk ten-minute walk around the block will be sufficient to wake you up. You might use the route you take as one of your memory 'journeys' so that you could 'revise as you walk' (**Ch 12**).

GO And now . . .

3.1 **Dispel negative thoughts.** Rather than dwelling on past failures or errors, focus on how this time things will be different, because of your fresh approach having taken on board the feedback provided to you (**Ch 10**).

3.2 **Try to become more aware of time.** Challenge yourself to estimate time-spans. Is what you imagine to be ten minutes more like twenty? If you are widely out in your estimation, then this might be a factor in your time management on the exam day.

3.3 **Practise writing against the clock.** Calculate the exact time that you'd have in the exam to respond to one question and write a practice answer within that time allocation. This will give you a better idea of how much you can write in the time and alert you to strategies for giving the best answer you can; for example, by limiting the length of your introduction so that you have more time to devote to constructing the analysis or argument that the examiner wants to read.

Study styles

4 Your learning personality

How to identify and capitalise on your preferred learning style

Your revision will be more effective if you know how you learn best and how this relates to your personality. This will help you to think more perceptively about how to tackle particular learning activities. This chapter explores approaches to determining your preferred learning style.

Key topics:
→ Why knowing your learning style is important
→ An introduction to the Myers-Briggs Type Inventory

Key terms
Existentialist   Extrovert   Introvert   Kinesthetic   Learning style
MBTI   Multiple Intelligence

In real-world employment, a growth industry has developed in identifying employees' learning styles. The aim is to help managers identify the best way to approach the training of their employees and to build more effective work teams. In education, the potential for adjusting study technique to produce a better fit with learning styles and preferences has long been recognised, and this is increasingly being promoted in university teaching.

→ Why knowing your learning style is important

Put simply, the potential exists to use information about your learning style to perform better at university. This will help you to:

● identify your academic strengths and weaknesses;
● help you study more effectively;
● approach problem-solving more flexibly, especially when working with others.

Your natural learning style has already evolved significantly by the age of three and, as you go through your education, your style is influenced by the behaviours you learn. Trying to be true to your own learning style may have been difficult in the mass education system of school, where there is little scope to adjust to the predominant teaching methods. Your ability to favour your personal learning style may have been placed 'on hold' until you reach university, where you have more choice over what you learn and how you learn it.

However, as a student, for some activities you can probably adopt an approach that is suited to the subject and methods of teaching and assessment. If you know what your learning preferences are, you will be better placed to adopt a method that is suited to your 'natural' learning style.

→ An introduction to the Myers-Briggs Type Inventory

The Myers-Briggs Type Inventory (MBTI) has become a benchmark for identifying personality and learning-style attributes. It has been much used by managers, trainers and human resource specialists to explore team-building. Look at Table 4.1 and do the short quiz that will help you to decide what your particular personality/learning type is. The 16 personality type categories are derived from a list of four pairs of items. You are asked to opt for one or the other. If you have difficulty selecting, then think about how you liked to do things as a child below the age of 10: that preference probably represents your underlying personality type. Once you have completed this quiz and found your category combination as a sequence of letters (for example, ENTJ), look at Table 4.2. This 'decodes' your style combination and its characteristics. Once you have identified your attributes, go to Table 4.3, which identifies some of the implications for your learning.

Table 4.1 Personality/learning self-assessment quiz. Adapted from the MBTI: there are four preference scales, with two choices in each – select what best describes you and tick the appropriate box in one of the double selections. Note the letters you have selected in the self-assessment grid below and use this code in Tables 4.2 and 4.3.

Preference scale 1 – how do you focus your attention and energy?	
Extroversion (E) ☐	Introversion (I) ☐
• Like participation and socialisation; motivated by interaction with others • Act first and think second • Energised by outside world and people • Impatient of tedious jobs	• Prefer one-to-one interaction; less comfortable in crowds • Ponder ideas before speaking/acting • Want to understand the world • 'Recharge batteries' regularly
Preference scale 2 – how do you assimilate information?	
Sensing (S) ☐	Intuition (N) ☐
• Focus on the here and now • Observe what is going on all around; with good recall of past events • Instinctively use common sense and seek practical solutions to problems • Improvise solutions based on past experience • Like clear information; dislike unclear facts	• Focus on the future • Seek patterns and relationships between facts gathered • Trust instincts and imagination to evolve new possibilities • Improvise solutions based on theoretical understanding • Not fazed by unclear facts or information; guess meaning on information available
Preference scale 3 – how do you evaluate information?	
Thinking (T) ☐	Feeling (F) ☐
• Analyse problem and logical impact of decisions objectively • Strong principles and need a purpose • Frankly honest rather than diplomatic • Accept conflict as a norm in dealing with people	• Reach decisions on basis of personal feelings and impact on others • Sensitive to needs of others and act accordingly • Seek consensus • Dislike conflict and tension
Preference scale 4 – how do you select your lifestyle choices?	
Judging (J) ☐	Perceiving (P) ☐
• Plan in detail in advance • Focus on task, finish and move on • Regulate life by routines, date-setting • Work best keeping ahead of deadlines	• Plan on the job • Multitask, good in crises, flexible and receptive to new information • Need flexibility; dislike being boxed in by arrangements • Work best close to deadlines

Self-assessment:

Insert your four preferences **in order** and then look at Table 4.2 to find your definition

☐ ☐ ☐ ☐
1 2 3 4

Table 4.2 **Personality/learning types (derived from MBTI).** Check your personality characteristics from the letter combination that you derived in Table 4.1.

Extrovert types		
MBTI type	Characteristics	
1	ENFJ	Friendly, outgoing, sociable and enthusiastic. Decide on basis of personal values. Empathetic but easily hurt; like to maintain stable relationships. Actively encourage personal growth in others. Attuned to others' emotions. **Keywords:** sensitive, innovative, optimistic, adaptable, resourceful
2	ENFP	Talkative, outgoing, curious and playful. Come up with new ideas, energise groups, proceed on the basis of patterns they see. May neglect details in planning. Enjoy experimentation and variety. **Keywords:** sensitive, innovative, creative, optimistic, adaptable, resourceful
3	ENTJ	Friendly, strong-willed, outspoken and logical. See the big picture. Demand much of selves and others. Natural leaders who organise people and processes towards completion. Develop systems to eliminate inefficiency. Less tolerant of people who do not come up to standard. **Keywords:** decisive, organised, efficient
4	ENTP	Friendly, out-going, humorous, flexible and unpredictable. Make decisions on logical basis. Ingenious problem-solvers. Tend to ignore routine tasks. Like to initiate change. See obstacles as challenges to overcome. Sparkle in debate. Good at 'reading' people. **Keywords:** logical, analytical, creative, imaginative
5	ESFJ	Active, friendly, talkative and energetic. Good at hosting. Can't handle criticism or conflict. Encourage teamwork to overcome problems. Work hard at detail and meeting deadlines. Intensely loyal, need to belong. Decide on basis of personal values. **Keywords:** organised, responsible, conventional, realistic, literal
6	ESFP	Warm, gregarious, talkative, impulsive and curious. Live life in the fast lane, good company. Like harmony in relationships. Flexible, respond to life as it happens. Like troubleshooting, dealing with problems in fire-fighting mode. Can galvanise others into action. **Keywords:** impulsive, active, sensitive, caring, unpredictable
7	ESTJ	Energetic, outspoken, friendly and productive. Get things done. Deal with facts. Assume leadership roles. Bring order, process and completion. Decisions based on logic. Direct, tendency to be blunt to the point of seeming impersonal and uncaring. **Keywords:** practical, realistic, down-to-earth, traditional, accountable
8	ESTP	Active, adventurous, talkative, curious and impulsive. Live for today. Deal with facts objectively. Brevity in explanations: give recommendation and move on to next problem. Less interested in theories, more in practical action to solve problem. **Keywords:** observant, practical, logical, fun-loving

Table 4.2 continued

Introvert types	
MBTI type	**Characteristics**
9 INFJ	Independent, thoughtful, warm, reserved and polite. Preference for patterns and possibilities. Creative, bringing originality and flair to work. Personal sense of purpose. Like to have identified goals. Work hard at understanding others, helping them to develop their potential. **Keywords:** productive, original, kind, deliberate
10 INFP	Reserved, kind, quiet, sensitive and dedicated. Deeply committed to work. Generally flexible except when values are violated, then take up principled stance. Creative contributions but sometimes take on more than seems possible, yet get it done. Hidden warmth for people. **Keywords:** creative, original, imaginative, flexible
11 INTJ	Autonomous, intellectually curious, aloof, imaginative and innovative. Decisions after impersonal analysis. Strategist, enjoying putting theories into operation. Reserved but critical of self and others; set high standards of competence for all. **Keywords:** analytical, logical, organised, definitive
12 INTP	Private, quiet, sceptical and curious. Prefer dealing with patterns and possibilities. Decisions based on logic. Interested in new ideas, search for logical explanations. Meet complex problem-solving as intellectual challenge. Enjoy theorising, analysis and understanding for new learning. **Keywords:** non-conforming, adaptive, unpredictable
13 ISFJ	Cautious, gentle, friendly and thoughtful. Make decisions based on personal values. Accept considerable responsibility. Interest in people, working for their interests. Like stability and dislike conflict. Uncompromising in beliefs held. **Keywords:** diligent, conscientious, organised, decisive
14 ISFP	Kind, humble, empathetic, thoughtful and faithful. Adaptable, interested in people, loyal follower, supportive team member. Like harmony and working in small groups. Prefer own space and time parameters. **Keywords:** adaptable, responsive, curious, realistic
15 ISTJ	Conservative, quiet, realistic and practical. Very reliable group member, renowned for accuracy. Decisions after looking at options. Work towards achieving goals. Like structured routine in daily life. Like to be of service to others. **Keywords:** precise, honest, matter-of-fact
16 ISTP	Logical, pragmatic, quiet, autonomous and aloof. Like seeking new information and understanding. Detached appraisal, decisions based on logic. Analyse information in order to solve organisational problems. Like to be free to implement solutions. **Keywords:** realistic, flexible, resourceful, objective, curious

Table 4.3 **Implications of the MBTI for learning.** From the letter code you identified in Table 4.1, mark your four types on the matrix below to see the traits that could impact on your learning. These are only a guide, but should help you to think about how to adapt to improve your learning.

☐ Extrovert (E)		☐ Introvert (I)	
Learn best:	**Challenges:**	**Learn best:**	**Challenges:**
● by discussion ● by physical activities ● by working with others	● studying alone ● reading, writing, researching ● any solo activity	● by quiet reflection ● by reading ● by listening carefully to lectures	● shyness in group discussion ● taking time for thinking ● fast lecture delivery
Recommendation: Try to revise with a study buddy; study as if preparing to teach someone else		**Recommendation:** contribute to discussions by writing down what you wish to say	
☐ Sensing (S)		☐ Intuitive (N)	
Learn best:	**Challenges:**	**Learn best:**	**Challenges:**
● if material can be memorised ● by step-by-step approaches ● by following practical applications ● from real-life scenarios	● impatient with complex situations ● lecturers rapidly covering topics ● finding out exactly what is required of them	● if given theory ● by focussing on general concepts ● by using insight not observation ● from general outlines	● reading instructions thoroughly ● lecturers who pace material too slowly (for them) ● find repetition/practice boring
Recommendation: move from familiar facts to abstract concepts; use multimedia techniques for learning		**Recommendation:** look for opportunities to use self-instruction modes, e.g. using multimedia	

☐ Thinking (T)

Learn best:
- by using objective material
- when course topics and objectives are clearly defined

Challenges:
- when lectures seem in illogical order
- outlining a logic order, e.g. in textbooks and handouts

Recommendation: seek guidance/explanation from lecturer if course appears to lack coherence

☐ Feeling (F)

Learn best:
- by relating ideas to personal experience
- by working in small groups
- by helping others

Challenges:
- abstract topics, e.g. those that do not relate to people
- lecturers who seem distant and detached

Recommendation: try to establish rapport with lecturer by asking questions, seeking more explanation

☐ Judgement (J)

Learn best:
- working on one thing at a time
- knowing marking criteria

Challenges:
- last-minute changes in syllabus
- timetable changes

Recommendation: build flexibility into work plans to accommodate unexpected changes

☐ Perceiving (P)

Learn best:
- on tasks that are problem-based
- when under pressure

Challenges:
- procrastination
- difficulty completing tasks
- impulsiveness

Recommendation: find novel ways to tackle assignments; break longer assignments into smaller sub-tasks

Three further well-known profiling instruments are introduced in Table 4.4, which provides a snapshot of the approaches used. The tip box on p. 44 gives references so that you can follow up any that you find interesting.

What do the results of these tests mean? First, it is important to recognise that all combinations have merit: there are no 'right-wrong' or 'best-worst' types in MBTI or any of the other systems you may try.

Second, it is important to recognise that the *process* of reaching a measured conclusion is important. Each of these systems helps you analyse how you learn successfully, what your strengths are and how this information can guide you when thinking about how you learn best. Thinking at this deeper level will almost certainly help you to improve your study methods.

How you do this will depend on your diagnosed learning style, your subjects and how they are taught. Some examples might include:

- a person who finds they are 'ESFP' in the MBTI might decide to set up a study-buddy partnership as part of their revision effort (Table 4.3);
- someone who is has a pronounced bodily-kinesthetic intelligence or kinesthetic learning style (Table 4.4), might focus their studies on recalling real-life examples and case studies, or on remembering the details of specific lab or tutorial exercises;
- an individual who has a preference for sensing (Table 4.1), or has a visual learning style (Table 4.4), might translate their lecture notes into diagrams and flowcharts rather than lists. They may also find that their learning style impacts on their role(s) as team members.

Deep and surface learning

It has been suggested people are either 'deep' or 'surface' learners – for example, good at theoretical learning for long-term retention or, alternatively, better at short-term memorising of facts. This idea has been dispelled by researchers, who demonstrated that people tend to use either of these approaches strategically, depending on the context in which they are trying to learn.

Table 4.4 Three further approaches to categorising learning styles.
These approaches are all based on validated academic work and some are commonly used in employment interviews. See references on pp. 44 and 185 for more information.

Kolb cycle learning styles (Honey and Mumford, 1982)
Types of learner based on a cyclic model of the learning process • **Activator:** has an open-minded, unbiased approach to new experiences • **Reflector:** looks at issues from all angles, collects data and works toward a conclusion • **Theorist:** analyses and synthesises information that is then placed into systematic and logical theory • **Pragmatist:** likes to experiment with new ideas and theories to see if they work **Critique:** said to narrowly pigeon-hole people whereas in real-life situations individuals adjust their learning approach to the situations facing them

Multiple intelligences (Gardner, 1983, 1993)
A subdivision of intelligence into various categories that are said to be more or less pronounced in different people and which influence the way we process information • **Verbal–Linguistic:** shows good verbal skills; aware of sounds and rhythms • **Logical–Mathematical:** an abstract thinker seeking logical/numerical patterns • **Visual–Spatial:** good at processing visual images, accurately and abstractly • **Musical:** good with rhythm, pitch and timbre • **Bodily–Kinesthetic:** has good body movements; skilled at handling objects • **Interpersonal:** responsive to others' moods and motivations • **Intrapersonal:** aware of own inner feelings, values, beliefs and thought processes • **Naturalist:** has an empathy with the environment, living organisms and other natural objects • **Existentialist:** sensitive to deep issues about human existence **Critique:** theoretical basis perceived as abstract, but people can build on strengths for effective learning. This summary shows nine intelligences – others describe seven, eight and up to eleven used in different treatments

VARK learning preferences (Fleming, 2001)
A subset of learning preferences derived from Gardner's Multiple Intelligences and the Myers-Briggs Type Inventory (see text) • **Visual:** preference for learning from visual media; highlighting notes, using books with diagrams • **Aural:** preference for discussing subjects; attending tutorials and lectures rather than reading textbooks • **Reading–writing:** preference for text in all formats and language-rich lectures; converting diagrams to text • **Kinesthetic:** preference for experience using all senses; recalling by remembering real things that happened **Critique:** styles strongly related to learning input, strategies and outputs; treatment accepts that some people may have multimodal learning preferences

Additional reading on learning styles

Biggs, J., 1999. *Teaching for Quality Learning at University*. Buckingham: Society for Research into Higher Education and Open University Press.

Fleming, N.D., 2001. *Teaching and Learning Styles: VARK Strategies*. Christchurch: Neil D. Fleming.

Gardner, H., 1993. *Multiple Intelligences: The Theory in Practice*. New York: Basic Books.

Honey, P. and Mumford, A., 1995. *Using Your Learning Styles*. London: Peter Honey.

Practical tips for capitalising on your identified learning style

Think about what your learning style means for aspects of your studying. How might it affect these important processes?

- how you take notes in lectures and from texts;
- how you revise;
- how you study with others;
- how you express yourself in assessments;
- how you answer in exams.

Look at the big picture. Be aware that your preferred learning style may not be entirely applicable in some situations. Think about how you can modify it to meet such circumstances, perhaps by exploiting a different aspect of your personality.

Watch your lecturers. If students have different learning styles, it follows that this is also the case for lecturers. Observe the people who teach you and try to identify their learning style. This could be helpful in understanding why they present information in particular ways and may allow you to be more accommodating in dealing with the content of their lectures and tutorials.

Talk about learning styles. Discuss learning styles with friends to find like-minded colleagues with whom you could work collaboratively in lectures, research and study – especially if you are an extrovert who finds it difficult to cope with studying alone.

And now . . .

4.1 Compare different types of learning styles analysis.
Look at Table 4.4, read the material in each column and see
which descriptions seem to apply most closely to you. Having
considered the type of learner you identified yourself to be
under the Honey and Mumford classification, Gardner's Multiple
Intelligences or the VARK system, compare this with the identity
that you defined under the MBTI list (Tables 4.1–4.3). In what
ways are they compatible or incompatible?

**4.2 Consider ways in which your approach to learning may
need to change.** Does the preferred style or styles that you have
identified in this chapter match with how you learned in the more
prescriptive environment of school, college or other training
experience? Think about how you can move onward in terms of
adjusting to the university learning situation.

4.3 Find out more about learning styles. A list of text references
is provided on pp. 44 and 185. If you type any of the following
keywords into a search engine (for example, Google), then you
will be able to access further information on learning styles:

- Gardner's Multiple Intelligences
- Honey and Mumford's Learning Styles
- Myers-Briggs Type Inventory (or MBTI)
- Fleming's VARK (or VARK)

How to organise yourself and develop good study habits for revision

One of the distinctive traditions of university is that students are expected to set their own learning agenda within the confines of their course of study. This chapter covers practical ways for organising yourself for study, and ways of organising the material you need to support your learning, work for assignments and exam revision.

Key topics:

→ Sources of information
→ Organising your study space and your notes
→ Developing your skills
→ Getting down to the task
→ How to study actively

Key terms
Annotate   Chronological   Displacement activity   Practical

At university, planning your study and revision is very much up to you. This means that you have to organise yourself by thinking ahead, prioritising different study activities, balancing the time you spend on different topics, and making sure that you meet assignment deadlines and arrive at the exam hall well prepared (Ch 7). You may also need to decide what to learn and how deeply you need to understand it. An audit of what you will need and what needs to be done will help you to organise yourself. Examining learning objectives/outcomes (Ch 9) and taking account of assessment feedback (Ch 10) are good ways of judging whether you are hitting the right level with your work.

Most key information is given in printed format and students are expected to read this intensively in order to map out their own schedule of personal study. The most common places for finding this information include:

- **Course handbook:**
  - gives information about lecture topic, numbers of lectures, names of lecturers;
  - gives dates and venues of practicals, lab dates and tutorials;
  - gives reading lists for written work, for tutorial or practical work;
  - gives some guidance on subject-specific or preferred referencing styles;
  - may give some guidance on essay-writing as required in your subject area;
  - provides learning objectives/outcomes;
  - refers to marking criteria.
- **College/faculty/school timetable:** gives venues and times of classes and exam dates.
- **Noticeboards:** give important information, including late changes to printed information. You should find out where the relevant departmental, school and faculty notice boards are and consult them regularly.
- **Emails:** provide updates, reminders and other information. Group emails are increasingly used as the preferred means of communication with students. Thus it is essential to check your university email account regularly.
- **Virtual learning environment:** gives access to much of the above information, online. Course information may be posted on the electronic notice board or announcement page. Frequent attention to such announcements is vital for keeping up to date with what is happening on your courses.

Everyone needs a place to study, and, ideally, this should be a location that is exclusively 'yours'. However, if this is not possible, then investigate facilities such as study rooms in your department or study zones in your library. Alternatively, some people find that going to a public library or another specialist library on the campus provides the anonymity that allows them to study uninterrupted.

Working in a comfortable temperature with adequate light and ventilation is important. Your desk and chair should be complementary in height so that you are not sitting in a crouched position; conversely, if you are 'too comfortable' it is easy to drop off to sleep – easy chairs or on top of your bed are not recommended.

---

smart tip

Finding your 'own' space

This can vary according to your mood, the task or what's available at the time you are free. Some people are creatures of habit and like to lay claim to a particular niche in the library; others prefer home study. Whatever suits you, your learning style and temperament is the right approach. Don't worry if it differs from approaches adopted by others on your course.

Keeping papers and files organised is something that some people do intuitively, while others need to work hard at it. Each subject you study on your course will generate a lot of paper. Whether you receive this in hard copy or it is offered to you via websites or your university's virtual learning environment, you should keep it where you can find it easily and relate the content to other elements of the course.

You will generate other material yourself in the form of notes taken in lectures or notes you make yourself as a result of your research and further reading. It is important to record the sources of this information and be able to retrieve it when you need to use it. Table 5.1 gives practical ideas for organising the vast amount of information that you will gather.

Table 5.1 **Tips for organising key information arising from your studies**

Day-to-day 'housekeeping'
• Use time when you are at an 'energy low' to undertake routine clerical activities by writing up and filing your notes; use your 'high energy' time for intensive study.
• Be systematic – date everything as you receive or create it.
• Store your material in an organised way – invest in a series of large ring-binder folders, one per subject, with coloured dividers to section different elements of the course. This will help you to retrieve things quickly. You could arrange the subjects alphabetically or chronologically, for example. This is a matter of personal preference. The important thing for retrieval purposes is to be consistent.
• As soon as you start to use material from any kind of source, *always* note down all the reference information required to relocate the source should you need it at a later point. This information will also be needed should you wish to cite some of the information from this source in your text. This means that you should record all the information required for the reference system you may customarily use, for example, the Harvard Method of referencing.

Formulae
• Create a formula sheet for each of your subjects by listing *all* the formulae, along with a list of what the symbols mean. Keep this in your subject file in a position that can be easily located.
• Make sure that you have copied formulae down correctly. In particular, make sure that you have used capital (upper case) or small letters (lower case) and also subscript and superscript correctly. For example, in electronics V_{max} = peak of dc voltage, as opposed to v_{max} = peak of an ac voltage.
• By keeping your formulae sheets in a polythene pocket at the front of your file, you will prevent them from becoming dog-eared. If you have access to a laminator, then laminating your formulae sheet allows you to keep a hard-wearing reference readily accessible.

Electronically retrieved or created material
• Create separate folders for each topic within the course you are studying. This will make it easier for you to locate work.
• Save your material using a file name that will make sense to you even when you try to locate it several months later. It may be useful in some cases to add a date reference to the file name, for example: Dental caries 170406.doc
• Keep a back-up of all work done on a personal computer. This includes saving any electronic work that you have to submit so that you can produce additional copies if required to do so.
• Insert page numbers and the date on which you last worked on the document as a footnote (some packages will alter the date automatically every time you work on a document). This will avoid confusing different versions.
• Explore the software package you are using to find out how to print the file name and complete pathway in the footer section of your document.

Early on in your undergraduate career, it will help you tremendously if you review the learning and studying skills you need to develop. These may include:

- learning how to use IT facilities;
- being competent with the basics of a word-processing package – Microsoft Word is possibly the most commonly used package in most university facilities;
- learning how to use subject-specific software;
- keyboard skills;
- knowing the location in your library of books, reference materials and other subject-specific resources;
- being able to use your library efficiently by accessing its electronic catalogue and other electronic resources;
- being able to carry out Internet searches for reliable source material at the correct level;
- being able to organise, structure and write a competent piece of text appropriate to higher-level learning in your subject area.

Being able to do these things to some degree of competence will be of enormous value to you throughout your study years. If you feel that you need further assistance in any skill mentioned, then go to the relevant service in your university and make enquiries about courses or inductions that will help you to develop your skills. You will find information about how to find support services on the university home page. Look for:

- **IT support service:** for help with word-processing, software packages or keyboard skills.
- **Learning advisory centre:** for help from study advisers.
- **Library:** for a familiarisation or induction programme. For specific queries there will be an information desk where you can get help with your search or query.

Think about what you need to do, work out how much time you can allocate to finishing the task, decide how you are going to tackle the task and then get on with it. You may find that the first ten minutes is hard going, but then the ideas begin to flow.

Types of studying to be done

Studying is a multifaceted activity and one that differs according to discipline and subject. The first thing to consider is what you need to do to learn within your specialism. This could include:

- reviewing new material from lectures by annotating or rewriting notes;
- finding and reading related hard-copy material;
- finding material in a virtual learning environment or other web-based source;
- preparing or writing up reports or essays;
- preparing for exams.

Once you work out for yourself the activities that are necessary for learning in your field, then you will be able to assign the time and priority you give to each activity.

Recognise the importance of *thinking* about the subject material as a vital part of studying.

Displacement activity

This occurs when you find other ways of using your time to avoid getting down to work. Examples include:

- persuading yourself that you can study in the sun (or the pub);
- washing your car/windows/dog;
- going window-shopping;
- tidying your DVD collection or room.

Planning and overplanning are other kinds of displacement activity. Although planning is essential, there is the risk of overplanning: try to achieve the right balance between planning and productivity.

If the total number of displacement tasks or the time that you allocate to them is preventing you from making real progress with your studies, then maybe you need to make hard decisions about time management (Ch 7).

Asking questions

Although learning is up to you at university, if you do not understand something even after you have attended the relevant lectures, delved into the recommended texts and spoken to others on the course, then go to your department and ask to see someone who can help you. Departmental secretaries are usually good people to speak to first in order to find out about availability of academic staff. Otherwise, email your lecturer to make an appointment or to pose the question directly. Staff like being asked questions and within a few minutes may iron out the difficulty for you. This may also highlight to the staff member that a topic may need to be revisited with the whole class.

---

smart tip

Using your 'visual' brain

Generally, most people tend not to exploit their visual memory. If you use highlighters for headings and sticky place tabs on key sheets in your file, then this will help you find things more readily and also help you remember content because of the layout of the page or the positioning of notes within your file (**Ch 12**).

→ How to study actively

It's all too easy to go through the mechanics of studying by copying out notes or reading a chapter from beginning to end. While this could be *part* of the process, it's important to think about what you're doing and why. Table 5.2 lists some typical activities along with the questions you should be asking yourself as you do them. Being aware of these different aspects of studying will prevent you from working 'on autopilot' and will help you to internalise your reading and writing.

Table 5.2 Typical study and revision activities, with questions to ask yourself as you do them (see also tips in Ch 11**)**

Rewriting notes from lectures
• What are the key ideas?
• Do I need to reorganise these to create a logical sequence that matches my understanding?
• Is this taking up too much of my time? If so, try to take your original notes more neatly. If you think that rewriting notes helps you to learn, could you synthesise the notes into bulleted lists/flow charts/diagrams rather than lengthy sentences?

Making notes from texts
• How is the information organised?
• How can I identify the key ideas quickly to provide an overview? How can I restructure information into concise notes?
• How much detail do I need for: - learning about the topic?   - eliciting information for an assignment?   - revising for exams?
• What is the best method for framing my notes?

Thinking/reflecting
• What do I think about this topic? It's important that you don't just take what someone else tells you as the only approach on the topic. Think critically by questioning your own ideas. Be prepared to redefine your view in the light of new approaches, information or evidence.
• What should I be looking for - information or concepts? If information, how reliable is your source and can you cross-check from another resource? If concepts, what evidence is there for each viewpoint? How good is the evidence? What other evidence might be available? Where will you find this?
• Are any patterns emerging? Look for relationships or themes, such as: - cause and effect (reason and result);   - comparisons and similarities, contrasts and differences;   - threads of arguments, supporting evidence and counter-arguments;   - problem and solution information.

Working through problems and examples
• Is the answer sensible and are the units correct?
• Have I done what has been asked?
• Is there anything else asked for?
• Have I used the correct formula?
• Have I used all the information given in an appropriate way?

Practical tips for studying independently

Know your best time to study. You are at your most effective as a student at particular times; exploit this by doing intensive learning activities at these times.

Check out the hours that facilities are open. Find out the library, study centre or computing facility opening times. Plan your study periods around them if you prefer studying in these settings.

Plan ahead. Keep an eye on things you have to do over the following week/month and plan your time to fulfil all the assignments, lab and tutorial work on time.

Develop a personal filing system. Learn to be methodical in the way that you store notes, handouts and any other printed material within your filing system.

Think about the underlying principles involved in your learning. Keep your focus on the bigger picture and avoid becoming bogged down in the minutiae.

Take breaks. When working on your own it is essential to take breaks. It is also important to maintain your social networks, and taking regular short breaks with colleagues helps you to maintain perspective on your work.

Work with a buddy. Although studying is something that you may wish to do primarily on your own, coming together with another person on your course to compare notes, confirm understanding of more difficult points and discuss a set assignment can help the learning of all involved (Ch 6). This contributes to the consolidation of your learning and helps identify gaps in your knowledge.

Develop your professional vocabulary. For subject-specific and general language, it will help you to remember words if you write them down along with a simple definition. A small, cheap telephone address book marked off with alphabetical sections makes an instant glossary reference notebook. You can record new words/specialist terms easily in alphabetical order, which makes retrieval easier than if you had recorded these indiscriminately in a long list.

Reinforce your learning. You will need to be able to use the language of your subject appropriately and make sure terms are spelled correctly; you need to master key formulae so that they become second nature to you. This is a reflection on your command of your subject. Make a habit of checking through your glossary or formulae lists frequently so that you can make a conscious effort to learn how to spell the more difficult words or lay out formulae accurately.

Tackle tutorial questions. Do *all* the examples in a set of tutorial questions as part of your revision. Check your answers from the answer key, if provided. If you have difficulty in working out a particular solution, then ask one of your lecturers or tutors to give you some guidance – staff will often go to considerable lengths to help with difficulties. Once you are satisfied that you have the correct answers, file the tutorial sheets alongside the related topic notes.

 And now . . .

5.1 **Go through your subject handbook.** Note down all the topic areas that will be covered on your course. Use these topics as headings for the dividers for your files so that you have an allocated space for the notes that will apply to these areas when your receive them or compile them for yourself.

5.2 **Visit your subject departments.** Find out where the noticeboard for your year is; visit the department electronically by looking at its home pages to find out if there is any special area that provides routinely updated information for students; visit your virtual learning environment and explore any sites that have been set up to support your learning in your subjects. Familiarising yourself with sources of information at an early stage in the course will save you a lot of time later when you may be under greater pressure.

5.3 **Review your skills and learning patterns.** If you are 'rusty' on word-processing or not quite sure of how to search a resource database such as a library catalogue, then make it a priority to upgrade your skills. You can do this by consulting the appropriate facility or service in your university to access an induction or training course. Consult Table 5.2 and consider whether your approach to study activities is helping you to study as effectively as you might.

6 | Study buddies

How to work with colleagues to improve the revision experience

Teaming up with others as part of your study and revision effort is recognised as beneficial in many respects. This chapter explores some aspects of this 'study buddy' revision approach.

Key topics:

→ What is study buddying?
→ The advantages of study buddying

Key terms
Extrovert Introvert MBTI Study buddy

Revising for examinations is a positive experience in lots of ways. It heightens your understanding of your subject and allows you to make connections between different elements of the course. It needn't be a solitary activity and many people find that it improves their learning to work on revision with another person studying the same subject.

→ What is study buddying?

The study buddy concept is based on a mutual arrangement between two or more students studying the same or similar subjects, who agree to support each other in their learning by conducting joint study sessions within their revision timetable (Ch 8). Examples of suitable revision activities include:

● meeting together to work through tutorial questions, comparing answers and analysing the correct approach;

● studying a topic as individuals and then meeting at an agreed time to quiz each other on the topic;

- speaking to each other about a specific topic (even giving a 'mini lecture');
- sharing resources, such as missed lecture notes, handouts, website and textbook information;
- sharing advice about modules that one person may have passed but the other(s) not;
- working together on formulating answers to questions on past papers;
- providing psychological support when one of you needs motivating or stimulating to study.

This technique probably suits some personality types better than others (see smart tip below and Table 4.3). You'll need to decide for yourself whether it will be appropriate for you and, crucially, you'll need to find someone else who thinks the same way.

Personality types and learning styles most suited to study buddying

The MBTI divides people into either extrovert or introvert types, but individuals from both types can be suited to study buddy learning strategies. If, having carried out the questionnaire in Tables 4.1-4.3, you identify yourself as one of the following types, then it might be worthwhile trying this approach: ENIJ, ENFP, ENTJ, ESFJ, ESFP, INFJ, INFP, ISFP, ISTJ.

→ The advantages of study buddying

The study buddy approach works very much on the principle that two or more heads are better than one and that the process of working together to tackle problems, key issues or difficult areas can assist all those involved to learn more effectively.

- You can play to your strengths by helping with areas where you are stronger; and you can receive help from others to strengthen your weaker areas.
- Explaining your understanding to someone else can help to clarify the issues, process or technique in your own mind. It can also help the other party, who may learn better when things are explained by

a peer, because the language is less formal. They may also feel more comfortable about asking questions and seeking clarification or become less anxious about making mistakes.

- The pair or group dynamic can have a fun or competitive element that motivates some people; it can also generate confidence from knowing that others feel the same way as you.
- At a practical level, making an appointment to meet with someone else means you are more likely to tackle revision.

---

smart tip

Some practical ideas for buddy activities

Different partnerships work in different ways; here are some tried and tested strategies that students have found useful.

- Partners work on problems individually for a set amount of time and then reconvene to compare method and answers.
- Student A uses a white-board or flipchart to explain a process to partner, Student B. Then they reverse roles for another topic.
- Partners make up a 'bank' of short-answer topics by writing the question on one side of an index card and the answer on the other side. They test each other on random cards drawn from the pile.

Some advice worth remembering:

- Be sure that you don't spend too much time supporting others and thereby neglecting yourself.
- Make sure you and your study buddies focus on studying rather than chat.
- Don't assume that study buddying is an easy option to avoid the hard grind of studying alone – solo study may, in practice, be a part of the study buddy process.

?

How can you find a buddy?

The obvious starting points are friends from your class, members of a tutorial group or lab partners. You could also simply ask around before or after lectures or put up a request on an online discussion board. A lecturer might be willing to make an announcement on your behalf, asking anyone interested in forming a study group to come forward at the end of the lecture. You'll be surprised how many others will be interested in this activity.

Practical tips for working with colleagues to improve your revision

Arranging meetings. Pick a mutually acceptable time and locate a venue that will allow you to sit and discuss your work without disturbing others. Ensure that you turn up with all the relevant notes, calculators, worked examples and resources like dictionaries as appropriate. It's best to aim for a neutral venue. Groupwork areas may be available in your library or you may find study rooms in the library, department, hall of residence or student association. You may be able to take over tutorial or small lecture rooms (check the booking system first): these have the advantage of having whiteboards and flipcharts, which you can use to note down points or give explanations to each other. Ask your tutors or the departmental secretary if you can't find anywhere suitable – they may be able to help.

Set up ground rules. Agree on how you will work together, for example, start and stop times, and limiting coffee breaks to no longer than 15 minutes. Stick to what you all agreed. Make sure that it's clear that if anyone feels that the strategy is not working for them, then they can walk away from it without fear of offending the others.

Tackling the revision. Decide on the areas of study for each session and stick to these. Draw up a 'wish list' of aims/topics at the beginning of each session and cross them off as you complete them.

Seeking help. If, between you, an answer is not found, then go to your lecturer or tutor to ask for some guidance. Teaching staff are usually delighted when students show their interest in their topics by asking questions, so you shouldn't feel nervous about asking for some help. It is actually useful to lecturers to know when students are finding particular areas difficult, because they then know that they may need to review how they tackle it in lecture, tutorial or lab contexts.

Short or long sessions? Working intensively for a shorter time is often better than a prolonged session where people end up chatting about other things. Keep focussed.

6.1 Think about how you can set up a study buddy group.
Who might you approach? What subjects would the pair/group
cover? Where could you meet? How much time do you have to
work in this mutually supportive way?

**6.2 Decide which of your revision topics would best suit
the study buddy approach.** It may be more appropriate to
learn some material by yourself, and tackle other topics within
a group.

**6.3 Think about extending buddy activities beyond the
revision period.** These forms of working relationships could
apply at any time in your studies, not just before exams.

Time management

Time management

How to balance study, family, work and leisure when studying and revising

Managing your time effectively is important when preparing for exams and assessments. This chapter provides ideas for organising your activities and tips to help you focus on important tasks.

Key topics:

→ Diaries, planners and timetables
→ Listing and prioritising
→ Routines and good work habits
→ What to do if you can't get started on a task or can't complete it

Key terms
Perfectionism   Prioritising   Writer's block

Successful students tend to have the ability to focus on the right things at the right time, the capacity to work quickly to meet their study and revision targets, and the knack of seeing each task through to a conclusion. In short, they possess good time-management skills.

Time management is a skill that can be developed like any other. Your aim should be to balance the time you devote to study, family, work and social activities. Although you probably have more freedom over these choices than many others, making the necessary decisions is still a challenging task and Table 7.1 demonstrates just how easy it is for students' revision time to evaporate. This chapter offers some simple routines and tips that can help you improve your organisation, prioritisation and time-keeping. Weigh up these ideas and try to adopt the ones most suited to your needs and learning style.

Table 7.1 Some of the ways in which students' study and revision time evaporates. Do you recognise any of these types?

Personality type	Typical working ways . . . and the problems that may result
The late-nighter	Luke likes to study into the small hours. He's got an essay to write with a deadline tomorrow morning, but just couldn't get down to doing it earlier on. It's 2.00 a.m. and now he's panicking. Because the library's shut, he can't find a reference to support one of his points; he's so tired he won't be able to review his writing and correct the punctuation and grammatical errors; and he feels so shattered that he'll probably sleep in and miss the 9.00 a.m. deadline. Oh well, the essay was only worth 25 per cent – he'll just have to make up the lost marks in the summative exam . . .
The stressed-out non-starter	Shahid has to give a presentation to his tutorial group. Only thing is, he's so intimidated by the thought of standing up in front of them, that he can't focus on writing the talk. If only he had his PowerPoint slides and notes ready, he'd feel a whole lot more confident about this assessment, but he can't get going because of his nerves. Maybe if he just goes out for a walk, he'll feel better placed to start when he comes back . . . and then, maybe another cup of coffee . . .
The last-minuter	Lorna is a last-minute person and she can only get motivated when things get close to the wire. She produces her best work close to assessment and exam deadlines when the adrenaline is flowing. However, her final-year dissertation is supposed to be a massive 10,000 words, there's only a week to go and she hasn't felt nervous enough to get started until now . . .
The know-it-all	Ken has it all under control. The lecture notes are all on the web, so there's really no need to go to the lectures. He'll catch up on sleep instead and study by himself later on. Then he'll just stroll to the exam looking cool, get stuck in and amaze everyone with his results. Trouble is, the professor gave out a sheet changing the learning outcomes at her first lecture, missed out one of the topics (which Ken has revised carefully) and told the other students that the exam format now involves two compulsory questions . . .
The perfectionist	Pat wants to do really well at uni. She signed up for a vocational degree and has plans to land a plum job on graduation to start her climb up the career tree. She's doing OK in her assignments but not in exams. She wants her essays to be absolutely perfect and tries to do the same thing in exams. Often, she runs out of time with one perfect answer and two incomplete ones. Can she learn to sacrifice perfection for better overall performance?

Organising your activities more carefully is an obvious way to gain useful time.

smart tip

Advantages of being organised

If you organise your time well, you will:

- keep on schedule and meet deadlines;
- complete work with less pressure and fulfil your potential;
- build your confidence about your ability to cope;
- avoid overlapping assignments and having to juggle more than one piece of work at a time;
- be better prepared for your exams.

Diaries

Use a diary to keep track of your day-to-day schedule (for example, lectures, sports activities) and to note submission deadlines for university work or exam dates.

- Work your way back from key dates, creating milestones such as 'finish library work for essay', 'prepare first draft of essay', or 'finish revision for topic x'.
- Refer to the diary frequently to keep yourself on track and to plan out each day and week. Try to get into the habit of looking at the next day's activities the night before and the next week's work at the end of the week. A diary with the 'week-to-view' type of layout helps forward planning.
- Number the weeks, so you can sense how time is progressing over longer periods, such as a term or semester. Pinpoint exam dates.

smart tip

Choosing a diary

Some universities and many bookshops sell academic diaries that cover the year from September to August. This format will help you keep track of the numbered weeks and key dates in each semester or term.

Wall planners

This is another way of charting out your activities, with the advantage, like a timetable, that you can see everything in front to you.

Timetables

Create a detailed timetable of targets before exams, or when there is a large report or literature survey to write up. You could:

● break tasks down into smaller parts and space these out;

● schedule important work for when you generally feel most intellectually active (e.g. mid-morning).

A timetable can help you see the progress you are making if you cross out or highlight each mini-task as it is completed (see **Ch 7**).

→ Listing and prioritising

At times you may run into problems because you have a number of different tasks that need to be done.

It is much better to write these tasks down in a list each day, rather than risk forgetting them. You will then have a good picture of what needs to be done and will be better able to prioritise the tasks.

Once you've created a list, rank the tasks by numbering them 1, 2, 3 and so on, in order from 'important and urgent' to 'neither important

How can you decide your priorities?

This involves distinguishing between important and urgent activities.

■ **Importance** implies some assessment of the benefits of completing a task against the loss if the task is not finished.

■ **Urgency** relates to how soon before the task must be completed.

For example, in normal circumstances, doing your laundry will be neither terribly important nor particularly urgent, but if you start to run out of clean underwear, you may decide otherwise. Hence, priorities are not static and need to be reassessed frequently.

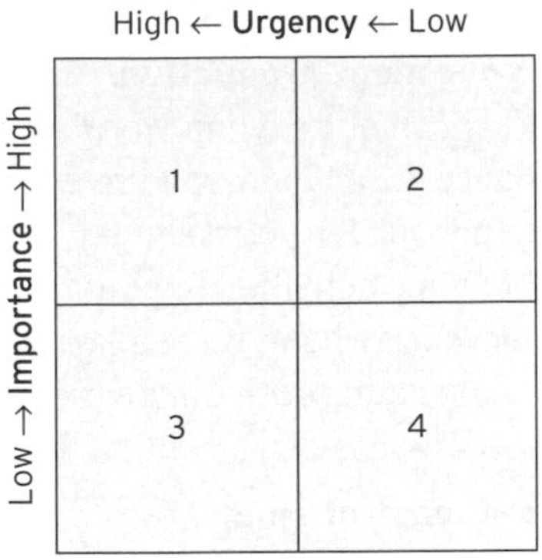

High ← **Urgency** ← Low

Low → **Importance** → High

1 2

3 4

Figure 7.1 **The urgent-important approach to prioritising.** Place each activity somewhere on the axes in relation to its importance and urgency. Do all the activities in sector 1 first, then 2 or 3, and last 4.

nor urgent' (see Figure 7.1). Your 'important' criteria will depend on many factors: for example, your own goals, the weight of marks given to each assessment, or the date of your exam.

Each day, you should try to complete as many of the listed tasks as you can, starting with number one. If you keep each day's list achievable, the process of striking out each task as it is completed provides a feeling of progress being made, which turns into one of satisfaction if the list has virtually disappeared by the evening. Also, you will become less stressed once high-priority tasks are tackled.

Carry over any uncompleted tasks to the next day, add new ones to your list and start again – but try to complete yesterday's unfinished jobs before starting new ones of similar priority, or they will end up being delayed for too long.

→ Routines and good study habits

Many people find that carrying out specific tasks at special periods of the day or times of the week helps them get things done on time. You may already adopt this approach with routine tasks like doing your shopping every Tuesday morning or visiting a relative on Sunday afternoons. You may find it helps to add work-related activities to your list of routines – for example, by making Monday evening a time for library study, working on whatever assignment is next on your list.

Good working habits can help with time management:

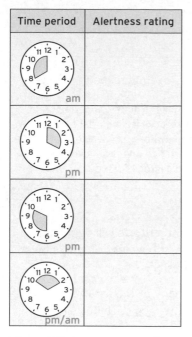

Time period	Alertness rating
am	
pm	
pm	
pm/am	

Figure 7.2 Are you a morning, afternoon or night person? Rate yourself (marks out of 10) according to when you find yourself most able to study productively.

● **Study intensively when you are at your most productive.** Most of us can state when we work best (Figure 7.2). When you have worked this out for yourself, timetable your activities to suit: academic work when you are 'most awake' and routine activities when you are less alert.

● **Make the most of small scraps of time.** Use otherwise unproductive time, such as when commuting or before going to sleep, to test yourself from revision cards on key formulae, dates or processes, for example.

● **Keep your documents organised.** If your papers are well filed, then you won't waste time looking for something required for the next step.

● **Make sure you have a plan.** Often, the reason exams and assessments don't go well is because there is no scheme to work to. Laying out a plan, preparing for an exam or writing an assignment helps you to clarify structure targets and to your efforts. Planning will save you time in the long run.

● **Extend your working day.** If you can deal with early rising, you may find that setting your alarm earlier than normal provides a few extra hours to help you achieve a short-term goal.

● **Ask yourself whether your lifestyle needs to change.** When you consider your use of time, you may realise that too much of your time is dominated by a single activity – socialising, caring for others, outside employment or travelling, for example. In such cases, you may need to make fundamental changes to balance your studies. Discussing your situation with a student counsellor might be able to help you decide what needs to be done.

People agree that one of the hardest parts of time management is getting started on tasks. Putting things off – procrastination – is all too easy, and can involve the following:

- convincing yourself that other low-priority work is more important or preferable;
- switching frequently from topic to topic, and not making much progress in any of them;
- talking about your exams or assessment rather than actually studying or revising;
- planning for too long rather than getting down to study;
- having difficulty starting a piece of writing (having 'writer's block');
- spending too long on presentational elements (e.g. the cover page or a diagram), rather than the 'meat' of the project;
- finding mundane TV programmes fascinating or being too easily persuaded to go out socialising.

If you admit to any of these symptoms, you may be subconsciously procrastinating. Becoming more aware of how you might be falling into this trap is the first stage in consciously avoiding it.

Delaying completion of a task, in itself a form of procrastination, is another aspect of time management that many find difficult. Procrastination is a special problem for those afflicted by perfectionism. Good time managers recognise when to finish tasks, even if the task is not in a 'perfect' state. At university, doing this can mean that the sum of results from multiple assignments is better, because your attention is divided more appropriately, rather than focussing on a single task. Tips for getting started on tasks and completing them on time are provided in Table 7.2.

Definition: procrastination

This is simply putting off a task. As the poet, Edward Young, wrote: 'Procrastination is the thief of time'.

Table 7.2 Ten tips for getting started on assignments and exam preparation.

1 **Improve your study environment.** Your focus and concentration will depend on this.
- Create a tidy workplace. Although tidying up can be a symptom of procrastination, in general it is easier to start studying at an empty desk and in an uncluttered room.
- Reduce noise. Some like background music, while others don't – but it's generally other people's noise that really interrupts your train of thought. A solution might be to go to a quiet place like a library.
- Escape. Why not take all you need to a different location where there will be a minimum of interruptions? Your focus will be enhanced if the task you need to do is the only thing you can do, so take with you only the notes and papers you require.

2 **Avoid distractions.** If you are easily tempted away from study by your friends, you'll have to learn to decline their invitations politely. Hang up a 'do not disturb' sign, and explain why to your friends; disappear off to a quiet location without telling anyone where you will be; or switch off your phone, TV or email. One strategy might be to say to friends 'I can't come just now, but how about having a short break in half an hour?'

3 **Work in short bursts while your concentration is at a maximum.** After this, give yourself a brief break, perhaps a short walk, and then start back again.

4 **Find a way to start.** Breaking initial barriers is vital. When writing, this is a very common problem because of the perceived need to begin with a 'high impact' sentence that reads impressively. This is unnecessary, and starting with a simple definition or restatement of the question or problem is perfectly acceptable. If you lack the motivation to begin, try thinking briefly about the bigger picture: your degree and career, and how the current exam or assignment is a small, but essential, step to achieving your goals.

5 **Focus on the positive.** You may be so anxious about your exams that this affects your ability to start revising. You may be so nervous about exams that you put the whole thing off. One way to counter this would be to practise – perhaps through mock exams. Focus on positive aspects – things you do know, rather than those you don't.

6 **In written tasks, don't feel you have to work in a linear fashion if writing for an assignment.** Word-processing software allows you work out of sequence, which can help get you going. So, for a large report, it might help to start on a part that is 'mechanical', such as a reference list or results section. Sometimes it's a good idea to draft the summary, abstract or contents list first, because this will give you a plan to work to.

7 **Cut up large assessment tasks.** If you feel overwhelmed by the size of a job and this prevents you from starting it, break the task down to manageable, achievable chunks. Then, try to complete something every day. Maintaining momentum in this way will allow you to whittle away the job in small pieces.

Table 7.2 continued

8 **Work alongside others.** If you arrange to work alongside others, you can spur each other on with sympathy, humour and the promise of a drink or coffee after each study period. See **Ch 6** for ideas about study buddying.

9 **Ask for help.** You may feel that you lack a particular skill (e.g. maths, spelling, or the ability to do a specific calculation) and that this is holding you back. Don't be afraid to ask for help, rather than suffering in isolation: consult a fellow student, lecturer, or skills adviser; or visit one of the many websites that offer assistance.

10 **Don't be a too much of a perfectionist.** We all want to do well, but doing your very best takes time – a commodity that should be carefully rationed so that all tasks are given their fair share. Perfectionism can prevent or delay you getting started if you feel your initial efforts need to be faultless (see 4 above). Also, achieving fault-free work requires progressively more effort, with less return as you get nearer to perfection. The time you need to spend to attain the highest standards will probably be better used on the next task.

Practical tips for managing your time

Invest in items to support your time management. Helpful items could include a diary, wall planner, personal digital assistant (PDA), mobile phone with diary facility, and alarm clock.

Investigate how you really use your time. Time-management experts often ask clients to write down what they do for every minute of several days and thereby work out where the productive time disappears to. If you are unsure exactly what you waste time on, you might like to keep a detailed record for a short period, using a suitable coding for your activities. When you have identified the time-wasting aspects of your day, you can then act to cut these down (or out). Those of a more numerical bent might wish to construct a spreadsheet to do this and work out percentages spent on different activities. Once you have completed your timesheet, analyse it to see whether you spend excessive amounts of time on any one activity or may not have the balance right. As you think about this, remember that universities assume you will be carrying out academic-related activities for roughly 40 hours per week.

Create artificial deadlines. Set yourself a finishing date that is ahead of the formal submission deadline for your assignment. That way you will have the luxury of time to review your work, correct errors and improve the quality of presentation.

Build flexibility into your planning. We often end up rushing things because the unexpected has interrupted a timetable that is too tightly scheduled. Leave empty slots in your plans to allow for the unexpected.

Try to prioritise the items on your 'to do' list. If you produce a daily list of tasks, then take time to think about how you wish to prioritise and order them through the day. You might adopt a numerical system or one using stars, for example.

(GO) And now . . .

7.1 Analyse your time-management personality. From this chapter, can you recognise any character traits that are preventing you from organising your time effectively? Might any of the 'Practical tips' help you manage time better? How could you adapt them to your own situation?

7.2 Experiment with listing and prioritising. If you haven't used this method before, test it out for a week or so. Make a list of all current and future tasks, assignments, appointments and social events. If the tasks are large, subdivide them into smaller components. Prioritise the list. Take special care to take account of events that depend on other jobs being completed. Now try to complete the components, ticking them off the list as you go. After your trial period, decide how effective the method was in organising your activities and helping you to ensure that tasks were done on time.

7.3 Declutter and reorganise your life. If you reckon disorganisation is a reason for lack of progress (Table 7.2), make a determined effort to tidy things up. Start with your room and study environment, and if necessary invest in files and boxes to help you organise things. Keep out only that which is relevant to current activities and carefully store the rest. Decide how you can better arrange your affairs to keep on top of routine tasks.

How to get yourself organised for exam study

Organising your activities in the run-up to exams is vital to ensure that you make the best use of the limited time available. Creating a revision timetable not only improves your time management but also helps you to balance your efforts among subjects and topics.

Key topic:

→ Setting up and using a revision timetable

Key terms
Active learning   Revision timetable

If your use of time tends to be haphazard, then a revision timetable will help to keep you on track with your studies. In addition, a timetable can help motivate you and provide confidence as you complete each topic. Used well, it can prevent you spending too much time on your favourite topics at the expense of others, and it can also ensure that you include relaxation activities to boost your energy and ability to concentrate.

→ Setting up and using a revision timetable

● Create a blank timetable. This will allow you to create an 'action plan' that gives details of the specific topics you intend to work on at any given time. The example illustrated in Figure 8.1 is based on six subdivisions of the day, with two potential study periods in each morning, afternoon and evening. If you prefer to use shorter or longer units of work, then modify the format appropriately, using a word processor or spreadsheet.

Figure 8.1 Sample revision plan for a student studying Environmental Sciences

Personal revision timetable
Sophie Pringle

Week: 12

Key to subjects/topics: Geography | Biomes + Diversity | Environmental Chemistry

	Monday	Tuesday	Wednesday	Thursday	Friday	Saturday	Sunday
Morning	Geog Lectures 1 & 2	Env Chem Topic B	Biomes + Div Week 3	Env Chem Topic C	Geog Lecture 8 & 9	WORK	Lie in
	Env Chem Topic A	Geog Lectures 3 & 4	Biomes + Div Week 4	Env Chem Topic C	Study buddy meeting Geog	WORK	Laundry
Lunch							
Afternoon	Env Chem Topic A	Geog tutorial	Geog Lectures 5 & 6	Biomes + Div Practicals	Env Chem Topic D	WORK	Biomes + Div Practicals
	Prep for last Geog tutorial	Break	HOCKEY	Biomes + Div Practicals	SPARE	WORK	Mock exam with Hilda
Evening meal							
Evening	Biomes + Div Week 1	Env Chem Topic B	EVENING OFF!	Library – look out past papers	SPARE (go out to union if up to speed)	Phil's birthday bash	Sunday tea with Mum and Dad
	Biomes + Div Week 2	SPARE	EVENING OFF!	Geog Lecture 7 (difficult)	SPARE	Phil's birthday bash	

- Now fix your start and end dates: these are the points at which you wish to begin revising and the precise dates when your exams are to be held. Print or photocopy enough copies of the timetable blank to cover this period and write in these key dates.

- Start to fill in the timetable by noting your *essential* non-study commitments, such as employment, shopping, cooking, travelling, team sporting activities and important social or family duties. If at all possible, these responsibilities should be minimised when you are revising, especially as the exams draw closer. Contact employers and others as far as possible in advance so you can warn them of your needs.

- Decide on the ideal number of 'sessions' you wish to study in each day and week, or are able to allocate due to your other commitments. Work out the total number of study sessions during the whole revision period and decide when they will be. For example, if you work best early in the day, you may wish to bias your studies to the morning slots that are available.

What's the ideal length of time for a study session? ?

Too long and you risk getting bored with the subject and losing concentration; too short and you won't be able to make decent progress. Figure 8.1 proposes sessions of about $1^{1}/_{2}$ hours in length, but you may wish to subdivide or combine these according to your preference.

- The next stage is to allocate these revision sessions to the different subjects or topics you need to cover. You may wish to carry out this process in two stages – first in a coarse-grained manner (say, dividing the total time among three modules), then in a finer-grained way (dividing each module's allocated time among the individual topics that were covered). Be flexible – you may wish to spend a whole day on one topic to get deeper into the material, or break another day up to create variety. In allocating time slots for revision, work your way backwards from the exam date, as this will allow you to ensure that you cover each subject adequately just before the relevant paper.

  Try to balance the time appropriately among topics or subjects. Your aim should be to give more time to 'difficult' topics than to

Avoid over-elaborating your timetable

Don't be tempted to procrastinate by taking too long pondering over your timetable or making it overly neat - it does not need to be a work of art.

'easier' ones, remembering that difficult or uninteresting material sometimes yields 'easy' marks when you have mastered it. As an incentive, you may wish to follow subjects you dislike with those you prefer.

If you aren't happy with the time available to study each topic when this process is complete, you may need to increase the total time you have allocated and reconfigure the sheets.

- In allocating time, recognise that you cannot work continuously if you want to study effectively. If you spend lengthy hours revising without any rest you may retain little because you aren't concentrating. Lack of focus and concentration will become worse if you tire yourself out.

Break up your work with relaxation, preferably involving physical activity. You may wish to set up 'rewards' (for example, watching a favourite TV programme or meeting your friends) - but only take these if you achieve your goals; if you do not, use these periods to catch up.

- Include some empty slots in your timetable to allow for unforeseen problems or changes in your plans. Your timetable should be flexible - if you lose time somewhere due to unforeseen circumstances, you should try to make it up later using these slots or switching slots from recreation to study.

- If at all possible, try to ease back on your revision load near the exam. Your aim should be to plan your revision to avoid last-minute cramming and fatigue.

Keeping tabs on your efforts

When there's a lot to be done, marking off the studying you have completed on your timetable, perhaps with a brightly coloured highlighter, can provide a visual indication of how much you've covered and hence boost your confidence and morale.

→ Using your time effectively when revising

Studying effectively is not simply a matter of giving over lots of time to the task: you must organise your activities well and use appropriate techniques to help you retain the material covered.

● Early in the revision period, focus on ensuring you have all the necessary materials to hand and that these are well organised – especially lecture notes and textbook information. Ask a friend for copies of notes if you missed a lecture, or download copies of summaries, overheads or slideshows. Pay special attention to these topics when revising, as you will not have the same feel for the subject if you did not attend the lecture. Look out your textbooks or visit the library as early as possible to ensure that you can reserve the books required. Avoid spending too long on this phase as a diversion from any real revision.

Avoid forgetting material you covered at the start of your revision

Try to make sure you do *something* for each subject or topic in each week. A task as simple as revisiting your distilled notes at intervals will keep facts and concepts fresh in your mind.

● Give your timetable the highest priority if conflicting demands are placed on you. If this means being a little selfish, then explain to others why you need to focus on your studies. On the other hand, don't be a slave to your timetable. Be prepared to be flexible. If you feel you are really making progress with a topic, stick with it rather than changing topic. Make sure, however, that you make up the displaced work at a later point.

● Recognise when your concentration powers are dwindling – take a short break when this happens and return to work refreshed and ready to learn. Remember that 20 minutes is often quoted as a typical limit to full concentration effort.

● Remember to have several short (5-minute) breaks during each hour of revision and a longer break every few hours. In any day, try to work for a maximum of three-quarters of the time.

- Use active learning techniques (**Ch 11**) so that your revision is as interesting as possible: *the least productive approach is simply to read and reread your lecture notes*.

Are you a morning, afternoon or evening person?

Identify the best time of day for you to study (p. 68). Focus your revision periods in these slots, and your routine tasks and recreation when you will feel less able to concentrate.

Practical tips for keeping your revision focussed

Make good use of your course handbook. This will help you find out about the structure of your exam and the content that will be covered. If learning objectives are published, refer to these to gain an insight into what lecturers will be expecting of you in the exam (see **Ch 9**).

Use past papers as a guide. Past papers will give you an indication of the style of questions asked. Try to modify your revision to accommodate the question style. Note carefully the structure of the paper and, especially if it has sections, whether each part will require a different approach to revision, such as memorising particular facts or a requirement to synthesise answers from several sources.

Work out, as best you can, how the exam will be weighted towards different topics. Bias your revision time accordingly.

Use lists to keep track of progress. As you revise, make an inventory of topics you need to cover, definitions you need to learn, for example. Crossing out the jobs you have completed will give you a sense of accomplishment and, from this, a feeling of confidence.

Test yourself continuously. The only way you will know whether you have absorbed and memorised something is to test yourself, for example, by trying to write what you think you have learned on a blank sheet of paper. If you leave it until the exam to find out, it may be too late to do anything about it.

Try to keep your mind working. If you find you 'drift away' after a period studying the same topic, try adopting the notion that 'a change is as good as a rest': you may find you can keep your attention up by shifting between subjects at appropriate intervals.

8.1 Create your own study timetable. The next time exams loom, create a blank revision timetable and use this to organise your studies as indicated within this chapter.

8.2 Compare study timetables with a 'study buddy'. If you can team up with a partner studying the same subjects, it might be valuable to compare your approaches to revision. When you have completed your draft revision timetables, discuss how they differ and why.

8.3 Focus your work by sitting mock questions. As you finish each section of revision, use questions from past papers to test your recall and depth of understanding. You don't have to provide a complete answer to a question to do this – an outline plan of an essay-style answer would be sufficient, for instance. On the other hand, if you can answer a complete question, you could pass this on to a fellow student or staff member for comment and learn from what they have to say.

Revision strategies

Focussing your revision

How to make full use of learning objectives, past papers and other assessment information

You can gain a deeper understanding of how you will be assessed from a range of sources. Studying these can help you to focus your revision and to enter the exam room better prepared.

Key topics:
→ Using learning objectives or outcomes
→ What marking criteria can tell you
→ Exploiting past papers
→ Learning from model answers
→ Setting your own questions and exams

Key terms
Learning objective   Learning outcome   Marking criteria   Mock exam
Model answer   Question-spotting

Universities publish a great deal of useful information that can help you to improve your exam performance. The most important sources are likely to be: module learning objectives or outcomes, marking criteria, past exam papers and model answers. As part of your revision, you should find out what exists and make full use of it.

→ Using learning objectives or outcomes

You will normally find the learning objectives in the module handbook alongside the detailed description of the curriculum (they are sometimes called learning outcomes). These statements represent the 'take-home messages' of the teaching and they state what you are expected to accomplish in your learning. This is then tested in exams and other forms of assessment. Despite the obvious importance of learning objectives, many students fail to look at them when studying.

> ### Compatibility between content and assessment ℹ️
>
> In an ideal world, there should be an 'agreement' between the learning objectives, the syllabus and the assessment methods. In other words, you should not be examined on something you didn't expect to have to learn.

Some departments lay out learning objectives as a series of bullet points relating to individual lectures (for example, 'Following this lecture, you should be able to . . .'). In other cases, the objective(s) may be framed in more general terms. Departments may also publish aims and goals for the entire module and it is also worth looking at these to place the course elements in context.

The relationship between exam questions and learning objectives is generally easy to see if you look at past papers and match up the exam questions with the relevant learning objectives and course material. However, be aware that the learning objectives may have changed through time – ask the module organiser if in doubt.

If you do not feel able to achieve a particular learning objective, it is worth checking with teaching staff. Perhaps you may have misunderstood the topic or the objective, in which case they may be able to provide you with further explanations. Also, a specific objective might be redundant because a lecturer was unavailable or made a late modification to their teaching – check!

→ What marking criteria can tell you

Marking or grading criteria provide an indication of what sort of answer would gain a particular percentage mark or grade in relation to a university's marking scheme. You'll probably find marking criteria in college, faculty or departmental handbooks or websites, because they tend to apply across many modules. However, they may also be published in each module handbook. Typical marking criteria include the following elements:

- **Content:** covering the range of ideas or information discussed and their relevance to the question actually set.
- **Depth:** referring to such aspects as complexity, detail, intellectual maturity and originality of argument.

- **Writing style:** relating to, for example, the logic, clarity and the quality of the English.

- **Presentation:** referring to the neatness and possibly also to the structure of your work.

- **Use of examples:** taking account of the relevance, accuracy and detail of those you quote.

- **Evidence of reading:** accounting for any reading around the subject you may be expected to do: this may come from the examples and sources you quote (not just those given in lectures).

- **Originality:** involving independent thinking (backed by supporting evidence and argument) or a new synthesis of ideas: these are dimensions that are highly valued, especially in later years of study.

- **Analysis:** including interpretation of raw data or information found in original (primary) sources.

Have a close look at your department's marking criteria. If you wish to gain high marks, these will tell you what standard your answers must be. Note, however, that although marking criteria provide a 'benchmark', the exact mark given will always depend on the topic and question and is a matter for the professional judgement of the academic and the external examiner.

Example of marking criteria

These are the marking criteria for a first-class answer (70-100 per cent) in a science subject at honours level:

- Contains all the information required with very few errors.
- Shows evidence of having read relevant literature and uses this effectively in the answer.
- Addresses the question correctly, understanding all its nuances.
- Little or no irrelevant material.
- Demonstrates full understanding of the topic within a wider context.
- Shows good critical and analytical abilities.
- Contains evidence of sound independent thinking.
- Ideas expressed clearly and concisely. Standard of English high.
- Written logically and with appropriate structure.
- Diagrams detailed and relevant.

→ Exploiting past papers

Past papers or sample questions are a vital resource. They may be published electronically on websites or virtual learning environments, or in paper form within the library. If you can't find them in these locations, ask staff or senior students for help. Use past papers to understand the structure of each of your exam papers, including:

- the format of answers expected (for example, essay, short-answer questions, multiple-choice questions);
- the number and style of questions you will be required to answer of each type;
- what the mark allocation is among sections or question types;
- the time allowed for answering;
- whether there is any choice allowed;
- whether the arrangement of sections forces you to answer on specific topics.

Next, use past papers or sample questions to understand the style being used. When looking at each paper, ask yourself:

- How much and what type of factual knowledge is required?
- How deep an understanding of the topic is required?
- How much extra reading might be required?
- How much or how little freedom will you have to express your opinion or understanding?
- Do lecturers have consistent styles of questions? Can you identify their different styles?

Use your answers to create both your revision and exam strategies (**Ch 11** and **Ch 15**) and the content of your answers.

---

smart tip

Linking past papers and learning objectives to enhance your revision

A possible approach is to photocopy past papers and then cut and paste all the questions into separate pages for each topic in the lecture course. By comparing the resulting groups of questions with the learning objectives and the material as taught, you can gain a much better picture of how you will be assessed, what types of question might turn up, and what type of revision needs to be done.

If model answers are provided, spare some time in your revision to read through these carefully.

Consider each question thoroughly *before* you read the model answer. Jot down a few thoughts about the way you would tackle it. Identify the relevant learning objectives that apply and think about the methods the lecturers are using to assess these.

Now read the model answer. This should be helpful in several ways, depending on how detailed it is:

- You should be able to grasp the language and style expected – for example, the type of introduction required, the use of headings and diagrams, what sort of things are in the conclusion.

- You should be able to evaluate the depth expected – for example, the balance between *description* and *analysis* that is present, the level of detail in any examples given, including use of dates, terminology and citation of authorities and authors. Especially at higher levels, university exams are more about using information to support a reasoned answer than simply regurgitating facts (**Ch 1**).

- You should be able to see how the different facets of the question have been addressed. Examine each part of the answer and identify what aspect it deals with, and how.

- If your lecturers also provide a 'bad' model answer, see what you can learn by comparing this with the good answer. Are you guilty of any of the errors highlighted by the comparison?

→ Setting your own questions and exams

After you have revised each section or topic, take the time to write out a few potential questions in the style of those seen in past papers. How would you set about answering your own questions? Write down plans as you would with an essay plan during the exam. This process helps you prepare mentally for sitting the exam. Consider it a bonus if any of the questions you predict come up in the real paper, but do not be tempted into question-spotting.

Avoid question-spotting

At worst, this involves predicting (guessing) a limited number of exam questions in the hope that they come up and revising that material only. This risky strategy is rarely condoned.

- Most examiners pre-empt it by making sure that questions are not repeated between exam diets and that patterns do not occur among papers. The chances of 'your' question coming up are very low.

- If your predictions are false, you will probably be unable to answer on other topics because you have not prepared for them.

- If there are subtle elements to the wording of the question, you may be tempted to provide the answer to your predicted question, rather than the precise one asked. You will then lose marks due to lack of relevance.

A 'mock exam', where you attempt to answer questions or a paper under realistic exam conditions, can help you in the following important ways:

- Testing your subject knowledge – and giving you early feedback about what you do and do not know.

- Helping you get into exam-answering mode and 'voice' – so that you can get rid of your rustiness before the proper exams start, can get going quickly in the actual exam and can start writing rapidly and appropriately.

- Timing your answers appropriately – so that you optimise marks and don't make the cardinal mistake of missing out questions through lack of time.

- Practising planning and laying out an answer quickly – so that you get used to the process of thinking rapidly through your answer before starting to write and, where appropriate, can check that you know the appropriate layout of your answer.

- Reducing the effect of nerves – rehearsing can help you perform better on the day. You should be less anxious if you are familiar with the act of answering.

Practical tips for focussing your revision

Keep the exam paper format in mind as you revise. Assess the style of questions at an early point and choose study methods appropriate to the style of questions you will encounter.

Use the learning objectives to check your progress. Your revision should include reading the learning objectives for each topic and ticking each off when you feel you know enough to be able to accomplish them.

Dealing with a lack of past papers. Your tutors may be reluctant to release past papers in cases where there is a limited pool of 'good' questions for them to use, as this might reward students who simply memorise answers. This is often the case where the paper is made up of multiple-choice questions. One way round this is to set your own questions, perhaps as part of a study group, and use these to test each other.

GO And now . . .

9.1 Make links between marking criteria, thinking processes and your study technique. Look at your department's marking criteria or the aspects noted on p. 84. Compare these with the levels of thought processes outlined in Table 1.1 on p. 6. This will help you appreciate the depth of learning required in your subject and level of study, and influence your revision and exam answers.

9.2 Assemble the important information about your next exam. Before revising for any exam, and certainly before entering the exam room, you should use published material to gain a clear understanding of:

● what the examiners might ask you;

● the format of the paper and questions;

● the depth expected;

● the length of the exam and its component parts;

● how your answers will be marked.

▶

9.3 Set up a mock exam as part of your revision. You may wish to 'buddy up' with someone else doing your subject.

- Choose a paper that you haven't studied closely (in fact, you may wish to hold one back for this specific purpose).
- Find a place to work that closely replicates the exam experience, such as a quiet library area.
- Sit selected questions or only one question as you see fit.
- If it seems appropriate, give a full answer to a question for which you have prepared. Alternatively, lay out your answers as plans rather than whole essays.
- If answering a full question or paper, allocate yourself an appropriate amount of time for answering - this should be as realistic as possible so that you can get a 'feel' for the speed at which you need to work.
- Afterwards, you could ask for a study buddy's or subject tutor's opinion on your answer. This feedback could be very useful. If you can't find anyone to do the checking for you, then critically compare what you have written with your notes.

10 | Exploiting feedback

How to understand and learn from what lecturers write on your work

When you receive back assessed work and exam scripts, these are usually annotated by the marker. It is essential that you learn from these comments if you want to improve, but sometimes they can be difficult to understand. This chapter outlines some common annotations and describes how you should react to them.

Key topics:
→ Types of feedback
→ Examples of feedback comments and what they mean

Key terms
Formative assessment   Summative assessment

There are two principal types of assessment at university: formative and summative. Formative assessments are those in which the grade received does not contribute to your end-of-module mark, or contributes relatively little, but which gives you an indication of the standard of your work. It is often accompanied by a feedback sheet or comments written on the script. Summative assessments contribute directly to your final module mark and include things such as end-of-term/semester exams, project reports or essay submissions.

→ Types of feedback

The simplest pointer from any type of assessment is the grade you receive; if good, you know that you have reached the expected standard; if poor, you know that you should try to improve.

If you feel unsure about the grading system or what standard is expected at each grading level, your course or faculty handbooks will probably include a description of marking or assessment criteria that explain this.

Written feedback may be provided on your assessed work. This will often take the form of handwritten comments on your text, and a summary commenting on your work or justifying why it received the mark it did. Sometimes the feedback will be provided separately from your submission so that other markers are not influenced by it.

Some feedback may be verbal and informal, for example, a demonstrator's comment given as you work in a practical, or an observation on your contribution during a tutorial. If you feel uncertain about why your work has received the grade it did, or why a particular comment was provided, you may be able to arrange a meeting with the person who marked your work. Normally they will be happy to provide further verbal explanations. However, do not attempt to haggle over your marks, other than to point out politely if part of your work does not appear to have been marked at all, or part marks appear to have been added up wrongly.

→ Examples of feedback comments and what they mean

Different lecturers use different terms to express similar meanings, and because they mark quickly, their handwritten comments are sometimes untidy and may be difficult to interpret. This means that you may need help in deciphering their meaning. Table 10.1 illustrates feedback comments that are frequently made and explains how you should react to obtain better grades in future. If a particular comment or mark does not make sense to you after reading these tables, then you may wish to approach the marker for an explanation.

Practical tips for dealing with feedback

Be mentally prepared to learn from the views of your tutors. You may initially feel that feedback is unfair, harsh or that it misunderstands the approach you were trying to take to the question. A natural reaction might be to dismiss many of the comments. However, you should recognise that tutors probably have a much deeper understanding of the topic than you, and concede that if you want to do well in a subject then you need to gain a better understanding of what makes a good answer from the academic's point of view.

Always make sure you understand the feedback. Check with fellow students or with the lecturers involved if you cannot read the comment or do not understand why it has been made.

Respond to *all* your feedback. Make a note of common or repeated errors, even in peripheral topics, so that you can avoid them in later assignments.

Get to know the standard proof-reading symbols and the abbreviations used by your tutors. Lecturers and tutors use a variety of words and symbols to suggest corrections and modifications. Most symbols will be standard ones used in editing (for example, ≡ placed under a letter means that it should be capitalised). If you find you cannot understand them, consult one of the standard texts for readers and compositors (for example, *Hart's Rules*, Ritter, 2005).

Table 10.1 Common types of feedback annotation and how to act in response. Comments in the margin may be accompanied by underlining of word(s), circling of phrases, sentences or paragraphs.

Types of comment and typical examples	Meaning and potential remedial action
Regarding content	
Relevance Relevance? Importance? Value of example? So?	An example or quotation may not be apt, or you may not have explained its relevance. Think about the logic of your narrative or argument and whether there is a mismatch as implied, or whether you could add further explanation; choose a more appropriate example or quote.
Detail Give more information Example? Too much detail/waffle/padding	You are expected to flesh out your answer with more detail or an example to illustrate your point; or, conversely, you may have provided too much information. It may be that your work lacks substance and you appear to have compensated by putting in too much description rather than analysis, for example.
Specific factual comment or comment on your approach You could have included . . . What about . . . ? Why didn't you . . . ?	Depends on context, but it should be obvious what is required to accommodate the comment.
Expressions of approval Good! Excellent! ✓ (may be repeated)	You got this right or chose a good example. Keep up the good work!
Expressions of disapproval Poor Weak No! ✗ (may be repeated)	Sometimes obvious, but may not be clear. The implication is that your examples logic could be improved.
Regarding structure	
Fault in logic or argument Logic! Non sequitur (does not follow)	Your argument or line of logic is faulty. This may require quite radical changes to your approach to the topic.
Failure to introduce topic clearly Where are you going with this?	What is your understanding of the task? What parameters will confine your response? How do you intend to tackle the subject?

Table 10.1 continued

Types of comment and typical examples	Meaning and potential remedial action
Failure to construct a logical discussion Imbalanced discussion Weak on pros and cons	When you have to compare and contrast in any way, then it is important that you give each element in your discussion equal coverage.
Failure to conclude essay clearly So what? Conclusion	You have to leave a 'take-home message' that sums up the most salient features of your writing and you should not include new material in this section. This is to demonstrate your ability to think critically and define the key aspects.
Heavy dependency on quotations Watch out for over-quotation Too many quotations	There is a real danger of plagiarism if you include too many direct quotations from text. However, in a subject like English literature or law, quotation may be a key characteristic of writing. In this case, quotation is permitted, provided that it is supported by critical comment.
Move text Loops and arrows	Suggestion for changing order of text, usually to enhance the flow or logic.
Regarding presentation	
Minor proofing errors sp. (spelling) ⋏ (insert material here) ⌐ (break paragraph here) ⁊ (delete this material)	A (minor) correction is required.
Citations Reference (required) Reference list omitted Refl	You have not supported evidence, argument or quotation with a reference to the original source. This is important in academic work and if you fail to do it, you may be considered guilty of plagiarism. If you omit a reference list, this will lose you marks as it implies a totally unsourced piece of writing.
Tidiness Illegible! Can't read	Your handwriting may be difficult to decipher. Allocate more time to writing out your work neatly, or use a word processor if allowed.
Failure to follow recommended format Please follow departmental template for reports Order!	If the department or school provides a template for the submission of reports, then you must follow it. If you don't, then you may lose marks.

And now . . .

10.1 Check out your department or faculty's marking criteria.
As explained above, these may help you interpret feedback and
understand how to reach the standard you want to achieve.

**10.2 Decide what to do about feedback comments you
frequently receive.** For instance, do lecturers always comment
about your spelling or grammar; or suggest you should use more
examples; or ask for more citations to be included?

10.3 Learn to criticise drafts of your own work. This is
equivalent to giving feedback to yourself and is an essential
academic skill. Annotate drafts of your own work – this is an
important way to refine it and improve its quality.

How to revise effectively through active learning

Active learning is the key to understanding and remembering course material for recall during exams. It involves thinking through concepts, ideas and processes, as well as techniques for effective memorising.

Key topics:

→ Basic active learning approaches
→ Preparing to learn and memorise

Key terms
Active learning   Chunking   Distilling   Learning objective   Mnemonic
Rote learning

Unless you are lucky enough to have a photographic memory, simply reading course material is a poor method for remembering and understanding it. Experience, backed up by research, indicates that you will remember things much better if you *do* something centred on the material (that is, 'actively' learn it). Moreover, this way of revising sometimes reveals flaws in your understanding that you may not appreciate when simply reading the material. There are many possible approaches to active learning and you should choose those that suit you and your circumstances.

→ Basic active learning approaches

You should probably use both the techniques outlined below for every exam.

'Distilling' or 'chunking' lecture notes

This involves taking your 'raw' lecture notes and reducing them to a series of headings and key points. This can be done in several 'sweeps', gradually reducing pages and pages of notes to just a few headings. An alternative approach to distilling is to reorganise your notes in grid format, as shown in Figure 11.1. The 'aspects' should be chosen to be relevant to likely exam questions. By creating this type of table you will force yourself to analyse the information you have been taught and hence understand it better.

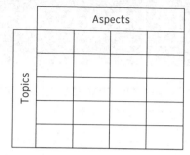

Figure 11.1 **A grid for reorganising notes**

The act of writing out the material when distilling or chunking your notes seems to help place it in a 'map' within your brain and aids recall. Another valuable aspect of these approaches is that they allow you to gain an overview of the topic – you can then appreciate where each aspect slots into the bigger picture. This may help you to memorise facts and place them in context within your exam answers. Finally, these methods are better than simply rewriting the material, because you need to *think* about the material as you transcribe into the new structure.

Answering past papers and problems

Looking at past exam papers is important to let you see both the type and scope of questions normally asked. The depth of answer required may not be so obvious, however, and if this is in doubt, consult subject tutors. You can take a variety of active approaches thereafter, from thinking through an answer in your head (weak); writing out an answer plan rather than a full answer (good); and setting yourself a mock exam or timed exam question based on a particular paper (excellent). If possible, discuss your answers or plans with subject tutors and fellow students.

Particularly for subjects requiring numeracy, problem-solving and doing examples are acknowledged ways of testing understanding and reinforcing what you have learned. Try to recognise patterns in the types of calculations and problems usually asked. Consult with subject tutors if you do not understand how to answer any questions.

Benefits of mock exams

These help you practise writing against the clock. Although time-consuming, this gives you an idea of how quickly you will have to work and how much you will need to condense ideas to fit the time allowed. They also give you practice in writing quickly and neatly by hand, which is useful because this is a skill that may have eroded due to the widespread use of personal computers.

→ Preparing to learn and memorise

Understanding concepts and committing facts to memory can be hard, especially when you find a subject difficult or unattractive, or there is lots of obscure jargon to learn. To give yourself the best chance to absorb the material, you'll need to ensure that you have prepared mentally, and that your working environment is configured appropriately. Here are some principles that might help:

- **You need to be ready to learn.** Make sure you are not preoccupied by thoughts of anything else.
- **Make sure your desk space allows you to focus on the work in hand.** Declutter your desk. If necessary, take your papers to a library or a similar place, where there is plenty of space in which to lay out your papers.
- **Make sure you pace yourself.** You can only study effectively in short bursts, so take frequent breaks to keep your concentration at a peak.

Getting rid of distracting thoughts

If you can't concentrate because something is 'bugging' you, try this technique: write all your problems and issues down on a piece of paper, which you now put to one side. Promise yourself that you will deal with these matters later on, but meanwhile will focus on your studying. This may sound rather silly, but it works for some.

- **You need to be determined to learn.** Avoid aimlessly reading material in the hope that it will 'sink in'. Convince yourself that you really want to learn. If you intensively focus on the material, fully intending and expecting to learn, then you will.

smart tip

Remembering facts

In any subject there is a core of knowledge that you should be able to recall, but, in general, you should avoid rote learning and try to think more deeply about the subject material. The focus should be on using the facts you have learnt, not on the facts themselves. The module learning objectives may give you clues about the direction that these 'deeper' thoughts should take.

- **Gain an overview of what you have to learn.** Knowing the context helps you absorb and remember facts. If you see the bigger picture, it's easier to fit the component parts into it.
- **Limit the amount you have to learn.** Condense the material into lists or smaller chunks. Split large groups of information into smaller parts.
- **'Visualise' and 'associate' to learn.** At its most simple, this means knowing how many items you need to remember. It could also include recalling a doodle on the page of your notes beside the text. More complex methods include associating facts with a familiar journey or location (see **Ch 12**).
- **Check your recall.** Don't trust to chance that you have learned the material – test yourself continuously (p. 114).

smart tip

Keep your revision interesting

Try to use a variety of approaches to avoid boredom during your revision. Experiment to see which method suits you best.

Practical tips for active learning

Further information about some of these tips is provided in **Ch 12**; which includes a range of other methods to aid recall.

Make your notes memorable. Use coloured pens and highlighters, but beware of overuse of emphasis and 'absent-minded' or purposeless highlighting, that is, when you highlight almost everything or don't really think why you have highlighted something.

Use concept or mind maps. These help to condense your knowledge of a particular topic. If you include drawings you may find that such image-based notes make recall easier.

Test your recall of diagram labels. Draw up important diagrams without labels, copy these, and then use them to test yourself from time to time.

Try recitation as an alternative to written recall. Talk about your topic to another person, preferably someone in your class. Talk to yourself if necessary. Explaining something out loud is a good test of understanding.

Prepare a series of 'revision sheets'. Note details for each particular topic on a single piece of paper, perhaps arranged as a numbered checklist. If you have the room, make your sheets into a set of wall posters. Pinning these up on a wall may help you visualise the overall subject area. Some people like to use sticky notes for this purpose.

Share ideas and discuss topics with other students. The act of explaining can help imprint the knowledge in your brain, and it has the useful side effect of revealing things you don't really know, even if you thought you did (see **Ch 6** for further discussion).

Make up your own exam paper. Putting yourself in the examiner's mindset is very valuable. Inventing your own questions and thinking about how you would answer them requires a good understanding of the material.

Memorise definitions. These can be a useful starting point for many exam answers. Make up lists of key phrases and facts (for example, dates and events) associated with particular topics. Test yourself repeatedly on these, or get a friend to do this.

Adapt your revision methods to your preferred learning style, using information gained from Ch 4. For example, if you feel you are a 'visual learner' (Table 4.4), consider using diagrams and mind maps to summarise your notes; if your MBTI type is ESFP (Table 4.2), recall experiences and examples to help you remember facts (Table 4.3).

(GO) And now . . .

11.1 Try out a new learning technique. Next time you have a 'low-stakes' exam or test (one that does not count too much towards an end-of-module mark), pick one of the tips listed above, and see whether it works for you.

11.2 Find a study buddy. Compare lecture notes and ideas for possible questions in the forthcoming exams. Together, assess and try out any of the tips in this chapter, especially if they might work better with two involved.

11.3 Think about the suitability of where you usually study. How might you improve the existing location? Is it working well for you? Should you consider trying somewhere else? What other places might be available to you?

12 | Memory tips and techniques

How to develop tools and strategies to help remember information and ideas

Having key facts at your fingertips is critical if you wish to approach exams with confidence. You will then be able to demonstrate higher-level skills in your answers, because you can focus on marshalling and analysing your knowledge, rather than struggling to recall details of your subject. This chapter outlines some ways in which you can train your memory to work for you in exams and in other situations.

Key topics:

→ Where memory begins in learning
→ Strategies for organising notes into memorable formats
→ Tricks for recalling facts and cues

Key terms
Acronym   Flash cards   Johari window   Mnemonic   SWOT analysis

Being in a position to recall information under pressure is important, both in relation to the 'building blocks' of your answers – the essential facts and knowledge of your discipline – and in relation to concepts arising from the deeper thinking you have done about the subject. Moreover, in many cases the exam 'questions' will ask you to apply your knowledge in an unpredicted way. If you lack the crucial facts and theoretical framework to be able to do this, then your marks will inevitably suffer. In some cases, being unable to recall details can lead to a feeling of panic in the exam that makes things even worse.

Few of us have natural 'photographic' memories and some struggle to retain information and ideas, especially in topics that we lack interest in or have difficulty understanding. Sometimes, also, it is the volume of material that has to be covered that makes remembering it difficult. However, you can gain in confidence, and also perform better under exam conditions if you learn some elementary memory 'tricks' that can kick into action in the exam hall.

→ Where memory begins in learning

While this chapter is about the memory tricks you can use in exams, it is important to recognise that the act of memorising begins at a much earlier stage in your revision – in essence, you need to be able to recognise what it is that you need to remember before you can adopt and adapt tricks to pull this information out in the exam. This involves the information-gathering and information-processing phases discussed in Ch 1.

The first step is to identify the content of your course, the key concepts of the subject within the themes that have been covered in lectures, tutorials, practicals and seminars as well as the topics that have been covered in assignments (information gathering). From this material, you then begin to synthesise organised revision notes that provide you with the facts and deeper understanding of the topics (information processing). For many people, this is an important preliminary stage to learning in that it provides a degree of reassurance that they have all the material required in a manageable

---

smart tip

Memory and learning styles

Appropriate memory techniques are closely linked to your personal learning style (Ch 4). For example:

- **Sensory or visual learners** normally have a preference for practical approaches involving the use of images.
- **Active (extrovert or kinesthetic) learners** tend to prefer to learn by physical activity such as manipulating materials.
- **Intuitive (introvert) or reflective learners** prefer theoretical and analytical approaches to derive the meaning that underpins what they need to learn.
- **Verbal (or read-write) learners** opt for word-based tactics.

The various approaches outlined in this chapter may resonate more with some learning styles than others, so it may be worthwhile analysing your learning preference as part of your preparation for revision.

form, but they would probably not yet claim 'ownership' of that knowledge. This point marks the transfer to the next stage of revision where you embark on active learning strategies to embed this understanding into your knowledge-base, so that you are able to retrieve and deliver the information in an exam situation.

→ Strategies for organising notes into memorable formats

For all students preparing for exams, there is a need to learn a considerable volume of facts – for example, dates of legislation, permutations of chemicals, stages in a procedure or sequences of events. However, it is important to recognise that university exams are not simply about information transfer from lecturer to student and then back to the lecturer. Thus, facts in themselves are not sufficient for most university exam formats. Instead, in your answers you need to demonstrate the understanding and analysis that distinguishes your ability to think critically (see pp. 5–6). A measured answer responding to the task is required, rather than one simply listing facts or providing a disorganised jumble of information on every aspect of the topic. This means that you need to create memorable revision notes that reflect your understanding of the way that the course – and hence the subject – fits together. Ways in which you can do this include the following:

Creating lists

This is the most basic technique of all. The idea is to distil your notes into a series of headings (see Ch 11). Doing this in several phases helps to imprint the knowledge and the end result provides an overview of your subject that allows you to place knowledge in its context. This method is particularly suited to those with verbal-linguistic or read-write learning preferences. Numbering your lists can be a useful memorising device (p. 113).

Making time lines

You can use a time-line (Figure 12.1) to plot the progress of events, a procedure or a development. Time lines can be drawn as vertical or horizontal. You might find these especially useful where a significant series of events have been referred to at different points in a lecture series.

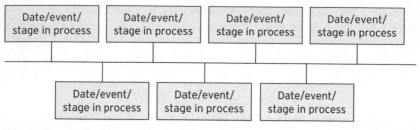

Figure 12.1 **Example of a time line**

Carrying out SWOT analyses

A **SWOT** analysis helps to analyse a situation, for example, as part of an appraisal of a case study or for a topic where a particular standpoint might be taken. It requires you to list aspects of the situation under one of four headings – **S**trengths, **W**eaknesses, **O**pportunities and **T**hreats. This analytical activity is an active learning technique that makes you think about the material more deeply. Noting bulleted points in a grid format, as shown in Figure 12.2, can be a useful memory aid that suits those with good visual recall.

Creating 'contrast grids'

This technique adapts the 'Johari Windows' method developed by Joe Luft and Harry Ingham (Luft and Ingham, 1955), and called after the first letters of their names. The method looks at pairs of contrasting aspects of an issue or situation and organises information or viewpoints within a two-by-two grid. The original Johari technique was designed to aid self-assessment of personality, but the technique can be used for other contexts (see Figure 12.3).

Organising complex information in grids

Tables and grids are good devices for helping to analyse systematically complex information that has been presented in a seemingly haphazard way, or that can be simplified by categorising the component parts. These grids or matrices can be particularly helpful in organising and remembering content for questions that require comparative and contrastive analysis. Figure 12.4 provides an example.

Strengths	Weaknesses
•	•
•	•
•	•
•	•
•	•
•	•
•	•
•	•
•	•
•	•
•	•
Opportunities	Threats

Figure 12.2 **Example layout of a SWOT analysis.** Each quadrant contains a series of bulleted points.

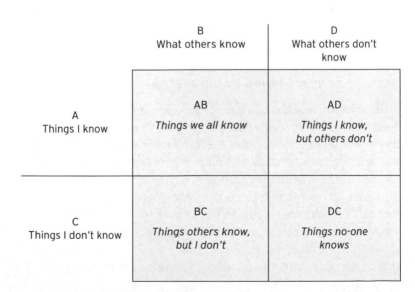

	B What others know	D What others don't know
A Things I know	AB *Things we all know*	AD *Things I know, but others don't*
C Things I don't know	BC *Things others know, but I don't*	DC *Things no-one knows*

Figure 12.3 **A 'contrast grid' used to analyse different viewpoints.** This example could describe a student reflecting on their own learning in relation to others in a group. Note the letter coding to show how each combination is arrived at.

	Viewpoint of individual employees	Viewpoint of Trades Unions	Viewpoint of industrial companies	Viewpoint of Government
Reduction in hours of statuory working week	• • • • •	• • • • •	• • • • •	• • • • •
Corresponding reduction in pension entitlement	• • • • •	• • • • •	• • • • •	• • • • •
Reduction in holiday entitlement	• • • • •	• • • • •	• • • • •	• • • • •
Reduction in number of days per annum as sick leave	• • • • •	• • • • •	• • • • •	• • • • •

Figure 12.4 **Example of a grid used to analyse viewpoints on an issue.**
In this case, the lattice of the grid allows the learner to note, in the relevant box, key points held by different stakeholders (listed along the top) on various aspects of a proposed policy (listed on the left).

Sketching concept maps (mind maps)

Another form of organisational diagram (Figure 12.6) is variously called a concept map, scatter diagram, spray diagram or mind map. In their most refined form, these are extremely visual, relying on colour and shape to produce an image that is both memorable and attractive. Some practitioners are able to use concept maps to encapsulate an hour-long lecture or public speech. For practical purposes, in exam revision and in the exam itself, the use of concept mapping has to be quick, legible and coherent. If you are happy with the strategy, the concept map can be a useful revision device as well as providing an outline plan of a response to an exam question.

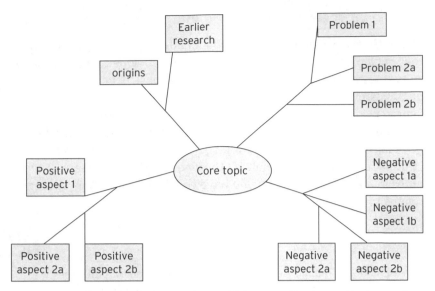

Figure 12.5 Example of a concept map. This generalised example does not include pictorial images, but adding colour, doodles and other visual links to the topics can help you to memorise the components.

Drawing diagrams

Diagrams can be created to show hierarchies, processes or relationships, as illustrated in Figure 12.5. They can also be used in your exam to provide you with an outline for a potential answer. Sometimes they can be formal representations that might be used within your answer. Diagrams are extremely useful to those with a visual or visual-spatial type of learning preference. However, take care when your diagrams are simply personalised sketches that are meaningful to you but possibly not to others. Although they can act as a memory aid to give you cues in writing your exam answer, they may not add significant value to the content.

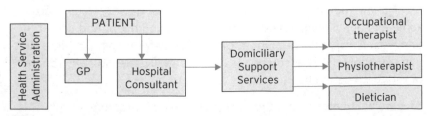

Figure 12.6 Example of the use of a diagram. This describes the organisation of health support.

Setting up poster or 'Post-it®' notes

This approach is useful for those who find that it helps their recall if they subliminally absorb information. It is a technique that particularly suits kinesthetic learners. The strategy is to construct a zone made up of posters or sticky 'Post-it®' notes on a wall in your hallway, bedroom, kitchen or bathroom to help embed the information into your memory, as part of your normal world. Thus, should your mind go blank in the exam, then you will be able to recall the missing information more easily simply by thinking back to the pattern of the notes in the context in which you have positioned them. This strategy relates to the 'pegging' of rooms described below.

---

smart tip

Using visual cues

In many of the models described here, the use of colour, different types of writing/printing, underlining, emboldening as well as use of layout, arrows and other symbols can influence your ability to remember the content. Some people go as far as to keep notes on different colours of paper or index cards to distinguish the level of their notes – for example, white sheets/cards for the longer, detailed version of notes on a topic pinned together with a coloured 'cover' sheet/card that contains topic headings and sub-headings for 'flash card' revision. In all of these strategies the aim is to capitalise on your visual memory as an aid to recall of concepts or written information.

→ Tricks for recalling facts and cues

The final stage of revision is to ensure you memorise the material ready for information retrieval and processing. Some of the above strategies for organising information will contribute to your ability to recall knowledge under examination conditions. However, there are some additional memorising techniques that you might find useful. Some need a significant amount of practice beforehand to ensure that you can apply the strategy under the potentially stressful environment of the examination hall.

'Mnemonic' relates to the Greek word meaning 'of remembering'. This term encompasses a range of strategies that work on the principle of remembering by association. Some examples are provided below.

Nonsense words

Typical ways of using mnemonics are to create 'words' that are made up of the initial letters of lists of items you need to remember. These are called acronyms. Thus, some people find it easier to remember the first line of the Periodic Table as the acronym **HHeLiBeBCNOF**, whereas others can remember this more readily as: **H**ealthy **He**rbert **Li**ves **Be**side **B**oring **C**ountryside **N**ear **O**pen **F**ields (hydrogen, helium, lithium, beryllium, boron, carbon, nitrogen, oxygen and fluorine). Another nonsense word acronym describes the purpose of research: **SCADAC**: **S**ystematic **C**ollection and **A**nalysis of **D**ata for **A**ction and **C**hange.

Rhymes

From folklore, there are many established rhymes that can be used to aid recall. For example: 'Thirty days hath September, April, June and November . . .'. However, it is possible to make up your own rhymes either as a kind of doggerel verse or sung to some common 'nursery rhyme' type of tune.

Spelling tricks

Clearly, it does not represent your abilities very well if you misspell words that are key to your study. Therefore, it is important to devise strategies to help ensure that you use the correct form in your written work. For example, architects and designers, might need to distinguish between the 'storeys' (levels of a building) or 'stories' (tales). It may be easier to remember the one that they usually want is 'storeys' because it contains the word 'store' and a store usually has different levels. Similarly, students of accountancy might find it difficult to remember how to spell 'debt' and 'debit' and they might find it helpful to remember that 'debit' rhymes with 'credit'. You will be able to design your own spelling tips if you keep a note of any rhymes or characteristics that you encounter.

Journey 'pegs'

In this approach you have to think of a fairly long journey with which you are reasonably familiar. The preliminary work that has to be done is to identify staging posts on the journey corresponding to the number of points that you need to remember. The strategy is then to 'map' the facts by relating each memory point to a staging post on the journey. This works from the principle of association where the different elements to be remembered are 'pegged' onto the known journey.

Special place 'pegs'

This is another strategy that relies on pegging the unfamiliar onto the familiar. You need to imagine a room, a picture or a view that is familiar to you and you select key items of furniture or features in the picture or view to associate with the factual elements that you need to recall. In the exam, you simply visualise the situation and then recall the items that you 'pegged' to them. A further refinement is to create a story around the image so, for example, you go into the room and switch on the lamp (West Germany), move over to the television (France) and switch that on also. You put your mug (Italy) onto the coffee table (Belgium) and place a cushion (Netherlands) on the sofa (Luxembourg) before you sit down. This 'story' could help you recall the six members of the original European Economic Community.

Story 'pegs'

Some people find that they can take the journey and special place pegs to a further level by creating a longer story that relates the events to the recall items. Here, people can base their story on a familiar tale, for example, 'The three little pigs' to remember Napoleon's path to taking over large tracts of mainland Europe – the house of straw (Iberian Peninsula), the house of wood (Italy) and the house of bricks (Russia). Alternatively, stories can be created by the individual and can be as innovative, ridiculous, violent or colourful as you wish. The object is to create a sequence of events that is meaningful to you and can easily be recalled along with the related associations.

Is the effect in 'pegging' worthwhile?

Some argue that the effort put into creating these scenarios might be better spent on just learning the material parrot fashion and it is also suggested that these pegging strategies introduce an additional series of stages in the memorisation process. However, the technique responds to the learning styles of some people – if it works for you, then it is worth the time and effort, especially where more conventional memorising techniques have failed you in the past.

Numbered lists

Listing is a basic revision tool (p. 105) and for people who like to learn in a linear fashion the use of numbered lists can be especially helpful. This is most valuable where there is a sequence inherent in the facts, and when knowing the total for the list can be useful in identifying whether you have recalled all the facts you originally collated. Breaking up larger lists into main points and sub-sections can be useful, particularly if the layout of the page 'staggers' the information by indentation and numbering of sub-sets. This can assist you to recall the image of the page and the list layout.

Logic rituals

For most of us, there are key things that we simply find it difficult to remember time after time. However, if you can identify some ritual of logic that you can apply each time, then you do have a way of unblocking that elusive piece of information. For example, the chemistry student who cannot remember how to calculate the density of liquid, can recall the units of density, grams (mass) per millilitre (volume), which helps her to remember that density is calculated as mass over volume.

Practical tips for memorising for exams

Practise, practise, practise. There is simply no substitute for going over the material and/or your memory aids again and again.

Practise mnemonics. You should be able to rattle them off without difficulty – but of course you must be able to recollect what the mnemonic represents.

Practise using memory journey, special place and personal story 'peg' strategies. If these appeal, give yourself some practice in using this strategy before you go into the exam.

Practise recalling and writing quickly. As students increasingly type their assignments and work from pre-printed handouts in lectures, there are fewer opportunities to practise remembering and writing at speed, skills that are critical to answering questions against the clock in an exam. By rapidly scribbling down your memory cues, you can also work on developing the skill of writing quickly as part of your revision.

Review what you have learned. If anything is the key to memorising, this is it. Don't just rely on the vague hope that you will be able to recall something – check that you can, and check frequently. If these 'self-tests' indicate that you can't recall everything, go back and start again. This repeated activity works to imprint the knowledge – and if it works, you will *know* that you know the material. Here's a possible method to try:

1 Read the material and, as you do this, write it out in list form, focussing fully on each point, trying hard to remember it. Note the number of items on the list.

2 Turn over the list and remove all clues about it (for example, close your textbook).

3 Immediately, rewrite the list. If you can't remember everything, go back to point (1) and start again until you can rewrite the list completely.

4 Do something else for 5 minutes, then rewrite the list without clues. If you can't remember everything, go back to point (1) again.

5 Do something else for an hour, then rewrite the list. If you can't remember everything, go back to point (1) again.

6 After 24 hours, again try to rewrite the list. If you can't remember everything, go back to point (1) again.

This method also works well with diagrams.

GO **And now . . .**

12.1 Revisit your notes with memory tricks and strategies in mind. Go back through your revision notes and identify where you could devise an acronym, or use another memory strategy to help you learn and recall information.

12.2 Challenge a fellow student. Ask them to race you in noting down the key points of a particular response within a fixed time period. This will give you both the chance to practise creating a quick answer outline based on your memorising strategies.

12.3 Swap memorisation strategies with friends. You could learn from each other and someone may have developed a strategy that is particularly valuable to your own subject, course or situation.

Stress management

13 | Dealing positively with stress

How to cope with the pressures of university life

Feelings of 'stress' represent a way humans have evolved to cope with difficult situations, by placing the brain and body under a condition of 'high alert'. Understanding these feelings will help you channel them so you perform better.

Key topics:
→ Identifying stress
→ What puts students under stress
→ Responding positively to stress

Key terms
Counselling   Nightline   Samaritans   Stress

Being a student exposes you to a number of events that can lead to stress – living away from home, giving up a good job to become a student, entering new relationships, organising your finances, deadlines and exams, to name just a few. Research shows that students learn better under a certain amount of stress, while too much, or too little, results in a weaker performance. This chapter covers general aspects of stress management, while **Ch 14** focusses on combatting exam nerves.

→ Identifying stress

Stress means different things to different people and involves a wide range of emotions and feelings, so an all-encompassing definition is hard to produce. Stress usually involves some form of external pressure, resulting in mental or emotional strain or suspense, typified by worrying, fretting and agonising. Most people feel stressed at some point in their life; equally, it is true that one person's worrying threat may be another person's stimulating challenge.

Recognising when you are under stress, or likely to be so, is important because it allows you to adopt avoidance strategies. Common physical symptoms associated with stress include:

- breathing difficulty
- comfort eating
- diarrhoea
- dry mouth
- fatigue
- feeling of panic
- food cravings
- headaches
- muscle pains
- nausea
- shaking hand
- skin rashes
- sweating
- tightness in the chest.

→ What puts students under stress

In general terms, you may feel stressed when:

- outside influences are putting you under pressure to perform;
- too many things are being demanded of you at the same time;
- you are afraid of the consequences of failure;
- there is a difference between the way things are and the way you would like them to be;
- you have little control over events but care greatly about the way they might turn out;
- you have been under low-level pressure for a long period;
- you run out of time and have a task to do in too short a period;
- you fear that you will not achieve to your own high standards.

Behavioural changes during stress

Common changes you may observe include:

- acts of hostility
- attitude changes
- biting nails
- chattering
- displacement activity
- feeling of depression
- irritability
- lack of concentration
- lack of humour
- loss of appetite
- loss of confidence
- loss of libido
- loss of memory
- loss of motivation
- not being able to think clearly
- poor driving
- sleeplessness
- withdrawal from company

Feelings of stress come and go and are caused by different factors at different times, as illustrated in the 'stress calendar' shown below. Most students will have experienced some of the stress factors listed, and it may be helpful to think back and note that you have successfully negotiated your way through these periods and become more confident in the process.

Sometimes, however, stress factors combine to increase stress symptoms to extreme levels and possibly to colour your judgement. If you feel that this has become the case, you should seek help from the counselling service. Table 13.1 demonstrates one method of evaluating such combined stress factors, but you should rely on your own feelings more than the results of this or similar evaluations if you sense that you might benefit from receiving professional advice.

In the run-up to exams, a range of factors can lead to stress. Some of these are shown on pp. 121-2.

The student stress calendar

Likely stress periods within each term or semester are as follows:

First weeks (especially as a 'Fresher'):
- being homesick
- difficulties fitting in
- new relationships
- encountering new teaching styles
- queries about subjects being studied
- feeling of academic inferiority

Mid-term:
- academic pressure - first assignments due in
- lack of 'real' friendships
- financial problems
- difficulty in balancing social life, studies and need to work
- self-doubt

End of term:
- end-of-term exams
- time-consuming extra-curricular activities
- lack of sleep due to studying, family responsibilities, partying or
- unsocial employment hours
- more financial problems, e.g. with seasonal gifts, travel
- blues on homecoming if you were living away

Table 13.1 **Evaluating stressful events in student life.** This table provides relative grades for major stressful events. Tick any that apply to you at this time or that have applied over the last two years. Add the scores for each as given in parentheses, for example (39). If the overall total is greater than 150, then you should seek help as soon as possible. If an event that applies to you is not on this list, estimate its impact and hence its rating in relation to the other scenarios described.

Higher-stress events	Medium-stress events	Lower-stress events
☐ Death of partner or close family member (100)	☐ Financial difficulties (39)	☐ Change in social activities (29)
☐ Divorce between parents (65)	☐ Change of course of study (39)	☐ Change in sleeping habits (29)
☐ Death of close friend (63)	☐ Trouble with parents or relatives (39)	☐ Lower grade than expected (29)
☐ Major personal injury or illness (63)	☐ New girl or boy friend (38)	☐ Change in eating habits (28)
☐ Jail sentence (63)	☐ Increased workload (37)	☐ Change in number of meetings with family (26)
☐ Getting married (58)	☐ Outstanding personal achievement (36)	☐ Bad problems with car (26)
☐ Fired or made redundant from part-time job (50)	☐ First term at university (35)	☐ Too many missed classes (25)
☐ Failed important course (47)	☐ Change in accommodation or living conditions (31)	☐ Change of university (24)
☐ Change in health of family member (45)	☐ Argument with tutor(s) (30)	☐ Had to drop a course (23)
☐ Pregnancy (45)	☐ Fear of the overall exam experience and consequences of failure [score may depend on circumstances] (20–40)	☐ Minor violation of law, e.g. parking ticket (20)
☐ Sex difficulties (44)		
☐ Serious argument with partner or close friend (40)		
Subtotal	**Subtotal**	**Subtotal**
		Total
		Other events
		Overall total

Source: Compiled, with the help of Dr Nick Halpin, after material available from several sources that adapt the Holmes-Rahe scale (Holmes and Rahe, 1967).

The university environment

Common issues include living in conditions not conducive for focussed study. This could include being distracted by flatmates whose assessments are at different times; having noisy neighbours and being unable to concentrate or sleep; or simply having a desk space that you find unsuitable. The solution is to carry out your studies at a different location where these effects are nullified, possible a library, a friend's flat or, if living away, the family home.

Domestic duties and work

Your 'housekeeping' needs such as shopping, cooking, cleaning and laundry, can interfere with your ability to study, as can the need to earn money through employment. The solution to this type of problem is organisation. Carry out your domestic duties in advance and also when you know your ability to study is likely to be poor (see p. 68). Ask others to help you, if you can. Explain the situation to your employer and ask for your shifts to be altered – most will be understanding.

Relationships

These often come under stress when students are spending a lot of time studying and revising. Especially if your partner or friends are not at university, you will need to explain the situation to them and make arrangements for 'quality time' together that is slotted in to your study or revision programme. Other worrying events include illness or death of relatives, or parental problems, including divorce. Your course supervisors will be very sympathetic in these cases, and able to make allowances – but can only do so if you tell them at the time what has happened.

---

smart tip

Importance of friends at exam time

Research indicates that students with friends at university are less likely to drop out. This is not only due to the beneficial effects of companionship and 'problems shared', but also because 'study buddying' (**Ch 6**) is such a valuable activity. It is worth discussing experiences and feelings about exams with your friends, and if they feel the same way as you (which they probably will), to join with them to reinforce each other's study effort and technique.

Personal issues

Your own feelings and health can lead to stress. It's common to think that other students are cleverer than you are. You may also lack confidence that you will perform to the required standard. You may feel lonely because you miss friends and/or family, or because you are concerned that you do not fit in with others. Another difficulty is coping with illness away from home, and its consequences in terms of your studies.

Academic factors

For some, the academic side of university life can be stressful. You may be uncertain whether you have made the correct choice of degree programme. It is also common to have difficulty in coming to terms with new teaching methods, such as lectures and tutorials, and the lecturing staff may make invalid assumptions about your knowledge or abilities. They may expect you to learn by yourself without the detailed guidance you are used to; and they may expect a high standard of English and reasoning skills. You may worry that you could embarrass yourself in front of others in your class or group. For some, the sheer volume of work creates problems; others may struggle if they miss classes.

What if I feel really, really bad?

For some, the stresses of student life are such that they consider dropping out or even feel suicidal. Talking about your situation is the best way to counteract these feelings. You can do this anonymously and/or confidentially through:

- The Samaritans (**www.samaritans.org.uk**)
- Nightline (**www.nightline.niss.ac.uk**)
- Your university's medical or counselling services (**www.studentcounselling.org**).

These sources provide contact telephone numbers and 24/7 online guidance.

If you feel that any of these factors or events are stressful to you, or are likely to become so, then it is important to respond positively. The practical tips provided below include many suggestions for dealing with stress in an active and constructive manner. They are in no particular order.

Practical tips for dealing with stress

Try not to worry about things over which you have no control. If necessary, recognise your personal limitations. Accept life as you find it and try to find positive ways around each problem.

Share your problem. Simply talking about your problems ('verbalising') can help you confront them, put them in perspective or work out a solution, while bottling things up may make them worse. You might wish to open out your feelings to a friend; or talk to a receptive member of academic staff (who will have seen most problems before); or seek a session with one of your university's counsellors.

Find out more about your problem. There may be books available about your particular problem, and there will almost certainly be a website somewhere. You may be able to work through a solution yourself.

Learn to prioritise. If you are stressed because you have too much to do, make out a list and put it in order based on urgency and importance (Ch 7).

Put things in perspective. Look around you and see how others are coping. There is always someone worse off than you are, and some people battle through against amazing odds. If they can manage, why not you?

Try to forget about your problem. Some problems (not all, certainly) simply disappear with time as events move on or circumstances change. What was a problem on Friday morning may have disappeared by Monday morning. Go out to the cinema for some escapism, get some sleep and see how you feel in the morning. Some people successfully put their problems to one side by writing them in a list and promising to deal with them after their assessment is complete or exams are finished.

Try not to be a perfectionist. Accept a lesser standard if this means your life is more balanced.

Confront your problem. OK, so you have a tough exam to revise for by the end of the week and it is causing you grief. Well, start revising. Apply the strategies explained in Ch 7, Ch 9, Ch 11 and Ch 12, and put in some hard effort. Running away from a problem means you avoid the issue rather than facing it.

Do something physical. This is great for removing the symptoms of stress. Go for a jog or swim or join a fitness class. This will provide an outlet for all the jangled nerves and hormones that your body has unconsciously prepared in anticipation of a stressful event. Try out yoga or similar methods of relaxation. Some people find these activities a great tool for de-stressing.

Don't be afraid to have a good cry. This is a very natural way to relieve stress in some situations – and this applies to both sexes.

Change your working pattern. If you are going out socialising more than you are studying, the remedy is obvious. If you can confess to slacking in other ways, then increase your work rate. Decide to work longer hours or work the same hours more effectively. Cut out activities that are preventing you from achieving your goals.

Try to manage your time better. See Ch 7 for more information.

Recognise that you can't please everyone. Accept that you may have to act selfishly or in a focussed way at times. You may find that others are far more accommodating than you thought they would be, if you simply explain and apologise.

Treat yourself. Instead of feeling that you are always doing things you don't like, or find hard or take ages to complete, give yourself a break and do something you know you will enjoy.

13.1 If you can, make sure you influence things. You may be able to remove the cause of stress. For example, if noisy neighbours are causing you stress in halls, ask for a move to a different room or floor in your residence. Or if you are experiencing financial problems, ask the bank for a loan. This may require determination and assertiveness on your part. Putting the blame on others is tempting, but you may have the solution in your own hands.

13.2 Use your university's counselling service. The mere fact that a counselling service exists should tell you something: others have been here before. This service will be staffed by professionals, expert in their job. They will make you feel at ease; assist you to work out your own solution; and put you in contact with others who can help. You can rest assured that the service will be fully confidential and independent from the academic side of university life.

13.3 Make an appointment to see a doctor or nurse if your problem involves your health. In the past, you may have left this sort of thing to your parents, but now you will need to take on the responsibility. You may need to register with a local practice (ask around to see which doctors have a good reputation) or you could use your university's health service.

Combatting exam nerves

How to reduce anxiety and perform well under pressure

Turn exam anxiety to your advantage. Recognise that 'nerves' are your body's way of preparing you to perform at a higher level. Boost your confidence by having a 'game plan' ready.

Key topics:
→ Reducing the effects of lack of preparation
→ Dealing with perfectionism
→ Performing under pressure

Key terms
Invigilator   Perfectionism

Most people about exams, even those who normally perform well in them, so if you get anxious you are not unusual. Nerves are best overcome through confidence generated by thorough preparation. Even if you've studied hard, it isn't possible to know 100 per cent of the coursework, nor to anticipate what exactly will be examined – and apprehension about the consequences of this is perfectly natural. Instead of fretting about it, turn it to your advantage, by recognising that being nervous helps provide both the motivation to study harder and a surge of adrenalin that is the body's way of helping you raise your game on the day.

> **smart tip**
>
> **Always try to think positively about your exams**
>
> Time spent worrying is time wasted – instead, use it to your advantage by tackling the work. It's vitally important to believe that you can achieve something – and this carries through right to the very end of the exam. The last fact you learn and the last point you put down on paper might be the one that ensures you pass or takes you into a higher grade band.

Feeling ill-prepared is probably the most common reason for being nervous about exams. Many a student has experienced the sensation of panic that comes when they realise that they have probably not done enough studying during the year – and that the time remaining for revision has become very short. If this applies to you, make a resolution to space out your workload next time round, then determinedly try to maximise your return on the time remaining. If you apply yourself to the task with a positive attitude, and are willing to work hard, you will be able to achieve quite a lot in a short time. The following tips may help.

- When time is limited, effective use of it is vital. Create a revision timetable that helps you optimise your activities (Ch 8). Stick to it rigidly. Reduce all sporting and social events to a bare minimum and cut down on any employment you have taken on.

- Over brief periods, you can stretch your working hours – for example, setting an early alarm isn't something you might normally think of doing, but this can easily add an hour or two to each day.

- Spend some time with others in your class to exchange ideas about what's worth studying and to obtain quick answers to minor problems with coursework.

- Be strategic in your work and approach to the exam by following these steps:
  - Without taking 'question spotting' to extremes (see page 88), study so that you maximise the return on the time put in. Use a highlighter to pinpoint critical learning objectives from the course handbook.
  - Now make sure you have the framework and basic understanding to begin an answer on each of these topics.
  - Next, focus on the key facts you must remember.
  - Finally, and only if you have time, get into the detail and examples.

- Exploit the time remaining as much as possible, by adopting active revision techniques (Ch 11) and using normally 'redundant' time effectively. For example, try to do small chunks of revision when commuting or in the time between lectures – this all adds up.

Don't forget to exercise during the revision period

Although you need to find as much time as possible for revision, don't reduce your exercise routine to zero. Besides being one of the best ways of reducing stress, exercise helps you maintain a good sleep pattern. Even a brisk walk can reinvigorate your mind.

→ Dealing with perfectionism

Exams, with their tight time limits and tough marking criteria, are especially stressful for perfectionists. To counteract this tendency, focus on the following points before, during and after the exam:

- Aim to balance your revision effort, rather than focussing on one area to the exclusion of everything else.
- Align your revision efforts with the learning objectives, rather than your own perceived notion of what you need to know.
- Don't go into an exam expecting to produce a perfect series of answers – recognise that this simply won't be possible in the limited time available.
- Don't spend too long planning your answer – for example, as soon as you have an outline essay plan, get started.
- Don't spend too much time on the initial parts of an answer, especially the first sentence, at the expense of the main message.
- Concentrate first on getting all the basics across – markers are looking for the main points first, before allocating extra marks for the detail. You may wish to rehearse these at the start of your answer as insurance against running out of time.
- Don't be obsessed with neatness, either in handwriting or in the diagrams you draw – but make sure your answers are legible.
- Don't worry if you've forgotten a particular detail or fact. You can't be expected to know everything. Most marking schemes give a first-class grade to work that misses out on up to 30 per cent of the marks available.
- After each exam in a series, avoid prolonged analyses with other students over the 'ideal' answers to the questions; after all, it is too late to change anything at this stage. Put all your mental energy into preparing for the next exam, so that you are ready to face that challenge with confidence.

First, recognise that exams are to some extent a test of your ability to perform under pressure, and accept the challenge laid down by the system. To do this, you need to be well prepared and particularly to have practised. If you've done well in the past, draw confidence from this. Self-tests and mock exams (**Ch 11, Ch 16**) are a good way of getting into the right frame of mind. They'll teach you much about the format and timing of the exam, and help you develop good habits.

Exams represent artificial situations contrived to ensure that large numbers of candidates can be assessed together with little risk of cheating. There is a lot to be said for treating them like a game. If you understand the rationale behind them, and adapt to their conventions and rules, this will aid your performance.

Mind gone a complete blank?

We all face this from time to time and also realise that the key to remembering a fact, date or name is often to think of something else. So, leave a blank space in your answer paper and come back to it later. Alternatively, if you can't see any way to answer a whole question, try one of the following:

- Brainstorm connections from things you *do* know about the subject.
- Work from basics, such as natural subdivisions of the topic (for example, hierarchical levels, such as parts of the body).
- Ask yourself 'Who? What? When? Where? Why? How?' in relation to the key subject matter.
- Think diagrammatically: base your brainstorm on doodles and images – this may open up different thought patterns.
- Search for associations: read through the other questions in the paper – they may trigger your memory.
- Get on with other questions if you can – the subject material might unblock your memory on others that seem to be elusive.

Practical tips for combating the symptoms of exam anxiety

Sleeplessness. This is commonplace and does little harm in the short term. Get up, have a snack, do some light reading or other work, then return to bed. Avoid caffeine (for example, tea, coffee and cola) for several hours before going to bed.

Lack of appetite/upset tummy. Again, these symptoms are common. Eat what you can, but take sugary sweets into the exam (and/or drinks, if allowed) to keep your energy levels up. If allowed, take some water to avoid dehydration.

Fear of the unknown. Confirm dates and times of exams. Go through your pre-exam checklist (Ch 15). Check any paperwork you have been given regarding the format and timing of the exam. Take a mascot or lucky charm with you if this helps. In extreme cases, it might be a good idea to visit the exam room, so you can become familiar with the location.

Worries about timekeeping. Get a reliable alarm clock or a new battery for an old one. Arrange for an alarm phone call. Ask a friend or relative to make sure you are awake and out of bed on time. Make reliable travel arrangements, so that you arrive early.

Blind panic during an exam. To reduce the symptoms, try doing some relaxation exercises (see below) and then return to your paper. If you still feel bad, explain how you feel to an invigilator. Ask to go for a supervised walk outside if this might help. If you have problems with the wording of a specific question, ask to speak to the departmental representative at the exam (if they have left the room, they can be phoned).

Feeling tense. Shut your eyes, take several deep breaths, do some stretching and relaxing muscle movements. During exams, it may be a good idea to do this between questions, and possibly to have a complete rest for a few seconds or so. Prior to exams, try some exercise activity, or escape temporarily from your worries by watching a movie.

Running out of time. Try not to panic when the invigilator says 'Five minutes left'. It is amazing how much you can write in that amount of time. Write note-style answers or state the areas you would have covered: you may get some credit. Keep writing until the invigilators insist that you stop.

Needing a toilet break. Don't become anxious or embarrassed about the need for a toilet break. Put up your hand and ask to go out. Your concentration will improve afterwards and the walk there and back will allow you to refocus your thoughts.

Think positively. You can do this!

GO And now . . .

14.1 **Begin your revision early.** Good preparation breeds confidence, which counteracts nerves.

14.2 **Discuss how you feel about your exams with someone else.** It always helps to realise you are not alone. However, try not to dwell on your mutual anxiety - try to gain a boost from friendship in adversity and focus on the celebration you will have when the exams are over.

14.3 **Complete the exam checklist** (Table 15.2). Knowing you have everything you need will boost your confidence.

As
the
exam
approaches

Exam strategies

How to ensure you have the appropriate tactics

Assuming your revision has gone well, the main pressure point in an exam is time. Effective use of this resource through an appropriate strategy is vital to ensure the best possible performance.

Key topics:

→ Key information required for a strategy
→ Producing a strategy
→ What to do during the exam
→ Arriving well prepared

Key terms
Law of diminishing returns   Multiple-choice question   Rubric
Short-answer question

An exam strategy is effectively a plan for managing your time and effort during an exam. This is vital to optimise your marks, because rushing answers or failing to complete the paper are reasons why many students perform poorly (**Ch 16**). Having a clear strategy will also mean that you will be more confident going into the exam room and will address the questions in a more focussed way.

→ Key information required for a strategy

Each exam will probably require a different strategy. For each one, you will need to do some research beforehand, by finding the answers to the following questions:

● How long is the exam?
● How is the paper subdivided into sections and questions?

- What is the nature of the questions?
- What proportion of the marks is allocated to each section/answer?
- What restrictions on answering are there?

You can find out these details from course handbooks or staff. Past papers are another source of information, but the rules may change, so it is worth confirming that the format is still the same.

Exam strategies do not need to be complex, but they do need to be planned with care, and ideally in advance as part of your revision effort.

Example: links between revision and exam strategies

A common type of restriction in exam papers forces you to cover the full range of the syllabus by stating that you must answer one question from each of a number of sections, each covering a different subject area. As well as influencing your exam strategy, this type of restriction should also affect the way you revise.

→ Producing a strategy

The following is a straightforward method for an exam with a set of similar-length essay or short-answer questions:

- Translate the exam's total length into minutes.
- Allocate some time (say 5 per cent) to consider which questions to answer and in which order. Allocate another 5 per cent as a 'flexibility buffer'. Subtract these amounts (10 per cent) from the total time.
- Share the remainder of the time among the questions to arrive at an 'ideal' time for each answer.
- Think about how you intend to divide the time for each answer into planning, writing and review phases.
- Before going into the exam, try to memorise roughly how long you intend to allocate to each section, question and phase.

Example: exam timing

You have a 2-hour exam (120 minutes), in which you have to answer 10 short-answer questions from a list of 20. You might allocate 5 per cent of the time (6 minutes) to reading the paper, choosing questions and reviewing answers. That leaves 114 minutes, which means each question should be allocated 11 minutes, giving you 4 extra minutes for flexibility.

You might prefer a slightly different model to the above where you would review all your answers towards the end of the exam, rather than reviewing each immediately after you have written it. If this would suit you better, you will need to deduct a further 5–10 per cent from the total before allocating planning and writing time to each answer.

Papers with mixtures of question types require more complex strategies. Much will depend on your estimate of the time each type of answer should take: base your estimate on previous experience (for example, in mid-term/semester exams) if you can, and take into account the proportion of marks allocated to each type of question or section. You may also need to decide on the order in which you do the different types of questions. For example, in the case of a paper with a multiple-choice component and an essay section, you may wish to do a sweep of the multiple-choice part first, then the essays, then return to the harder multiple-choice questions.

Your strategy should be flexible, in case things don't turn out the way you planned them – but only make changes during the exam if you are certain of what you are doing, and why.

Table 15.1 provides some examples of how other types of strategy can be adopted to avoid problems experienced with exams.

→ What to do during the exam

- Quickly check the rubric at the top of the paper and that the questions are arranged as you expected.
- Look carefully at all the questions on the paper. You may wish to mark off the ones you feel you can answer well, or adopt some form of scoring system (for example, marks out of ten) for how well you think you can answer them.

Table 15.1 Types of unstrategic approaches to exams and how to avoid similar problems

The disorganised person	
Experience	Dora has lost the scrap of paper that she used to note when and where her exam was. She plans to arrive at the time and place she vaguely remembers and see if she recognises anyone in the queue. Her bus is late however, and everyone has already gone in. She arrives breathless at her seat, only to find she's forgotten her pen and it's an Atomic Physics paper rather than Edwardian history . . .
How to avoid this problem	Dora could: • have checked the details the night before; • have planned to take the earlier bus to allow for hold-ups; • have used a checklist (Table 15.2) to make sure she has everything needed; • speak to the invigilator, who can give her correct information; • be allowed to sit part of the proper exam, if she can still get to the right place in time.
The nervous exam-sitter	
Experience	Nadeem is totally consumed by nerves on the day of his big exam. He needs to visit the toilet immediately beforehand and then nearly throws up. In the exam, the words on the exam paper swim before his eyes and he can't make sense of the first question, nor any of the rest. The questions don't seem to relate to any of his course work. He rushes out of the exam hall, frustrated and anxious . . .
How to avoid this problem	Nadeem could: • reflect ahead of time on his view of exams – why he feels nervous – and try not to allow a spiral of anxiety to develop; • try to exploit his energy rush positively, for example, by brainstorming key points as soon as he goes into the hall, thus giving him confidence; • use relaxation techniques within the exam hall.
The 'get-me-outa-here!' student	
Experience	Graham would rather be anywhere else than in an exam hall. He rushes through his answers, then hands in his paper 30 minutes before the end and speeds over to the union bar to wait for his pals to come out. During post-exam discussions, he realises that one of his answers is incomplete and he hasn't even attempted section B . . .
How to avoid this problem	Graham could: • familiarise himself with the format of the paper before the date; • plan his time in the exam so that he uses all of it profitably; • use spare time for checking answers to ensure he has done as instructed.

Table 15.1 continued

The perfectionist	
Experience	Patsy has spent ages revising and knows the topics inside out. When she turns over the exam paper, she is delighted to find her ideal question and knows she can produce a brilliant answer. One-and-a-half hours later, it's nearly finished. Only problem is, she now has another two answers to complete in 30 minutes ...
How to avoid this problem	Patsy could: • do much the same as Graham, but also recognise that she will gain a better mark for doing reasonably well in all the questions, rather than extremely well in just one; • practise writing answers against the clock to improve her technique.
The mind-blocked writer	
Experience	Mike has prepared for the exam well, but when he looks at the question, his mind has gone a complete blank. He can't remember anything to do with the subject material and feels like leaving the exam straight away ...
How to avoid this problem	Mike could: • begin by brainstorming a topic he knows well, from a nucleus of information that he can add to, and relate this to the questions asked; • ask a departmental representative for a clue; a note will be taken of this, but it's better than writing nothing and it will get him started.
The laid-back dreamer	
Experience	Lin can't really be bothered with all the hassle of exams and the need for all that stress. At the start, she takes ages to choose a question and more time to think over her answer. In the middle, she finds herself dreaming of the summer vacation. Suddenly the exam is over, and she's only half way through her first answer ...
How to avoid this problem	Lin could: • focus on the exam and why it's important to her; • make a conscious decision to concentrate on the job in hand; • consider how much vacation time she will need to spend on revision if she fails.

What if the exam paper is differently arranged from your expectation?

You will have to rethink your strategy quickly. It will still be worth doing this, as the penalties for running out of time could be severe.

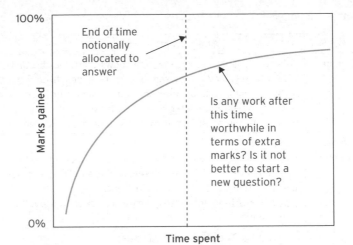

Figure 15.1 Why it does not pay to spend too long on any one exam answer.
The marks you gain tail off the longer you carry on writing. The extra return
will simply not repay the investment of time. Ensure that you start answers to
all questions to gain the 'easily obtained' marks, rather than wasting time
perfecting one answer.

- Think about your strategy, and the 'ideal' time for each question,
  then decide which answers, if any, might require more time, or
  might provide a good return in marks for a little extra time invested,
  and which questions might require less time. A potentially good
  answer should be allocated only slightly more time than one you
  don't feel so happy about. If you concentrate too much on any
  one answer, the law of diminishing returns means that you will take
  time from other answers without gaining compensatory credit
  (see Figure 15.1).

- Answer questions in a sensible order, which does *not* have to be the
  order they appear in the question paper. For example:

  - Some people prefer to answer 'fact-based' questions first, before
    they forget details memorised just before the exam.

  - Some people prefer to answer their 'best' question first, to get a
    good start to the paper. Others would prefer to do this second or
    even later, when they feel 'warmed up'.

  - Most people would agree that you should leave a question you
    feel unhappy about until the end: during the rest of the exam,
    ideas may come to you about it – note them down as you go
    along.

Example: benefits of answering all the questions expected

Suppose you had a paper where you were expected to answer four questions but only answered two, trying to do your very best in them. You might score, say, 75 per cent in each, but your total percentage mark would be (75 + 75 + 0 + 0) divided by 4, or 37.5 per cent (usually a fail).

On the other hand, if you answered all four questions, but perhaps less well, you might score 55 per cent in two and 45 per cent in the other two. Your overall percentage mark would be (55 + 55 + 45 + 45) divided by 4, or 50 per cent (usually a pass).

→ Arriving well prepared

Of course, the most important aspect of preparation is revision. No amount of exam technique will substitute for this.

You may need to register and, in some cases, pay for certain exams – check this at an early stage. You should also confirm the date of the exam, where it will take place, when it will start and how long it will last. This information may be given in the course handbook, posted on noticeboards, published on a website or within a virtual learning environment module, or may also be provided by the exam office/registry by post. However, it is *your* duty to ensure that you arrive at the right place at the right time. Write down the information. Double-check, perhaps by asking a member of the class who has independently found out.

On the day, plan carefully so that you can arrive in good time – this will allow for unforeseen circumstances and will help to reduce the anxiety element at the start of the exam (**Ch 13** and **Ch 14**). Going over a checklist of items to bring to the exam (Table 15.2) may also act to calm you.

In the exam room, always double-check the rubric at the top of the paper. It is not unknown for students to sit the wrong exam by mistake.

Table 15.2 Checklist of items to bring with you to written exams

✓	Item
❑	Writing kit: pens and pencils (plus replacements), ruler, rubber, highlighter(s), correction fluid
❑	Student matriculation (ID) card (staff will use this to check your identity)
❑	Special equipment: calculators, protractor, compass, digital recorder or similar for aural exams (check beforehand that you can use these aids properly), spare batteries
❑	Texts, where allowed for 'open book' exams
❑	Dictionary, if allowed (i.e. arranged beforehand with your department)
❑	Sweets and a drink, if allowed
❑	Clock or watch for timekeeping
❑	Mascot

Practical tips for time saving in exams

Don't over-elaborate your answer plans. Use simple forms of spider diagrams or mind maps to brainstorm and plan your answer (p. 108).

Use diagrams and tables in your answer. This saves time otherwise spent making difficult and lengthy explanations, but make sure they are worthwhile and that you refer to them in the text.

Use standard abbreviations. This will save time repeating text, but always explain the abbreviations at the first point of use. However, this is not necessary for 'standard' abbreviations such as e.g. (for example), i.e. (that is) and etc. (et cetera - and so forth).

Always keep your eye on the time. There is no point in having a strategy if you forget to stick to it. You may find it helps to take off your watch and put it where in can be easily seen on the desk. Some students find it helpful to work out the end times for each question beforehand as an aid to timekeeping. As the allotted period for each answer draws to a close, make sure your mind is on finishing your answer.

Consider speed of writing and neatness. Might you be wasting time by trying to write too neatly or using a type of pen that slows you down? Ballpoint and liquid gel pens are probably the fastest.

Conversely, are you writing too quickly and making your script difficult to interpret? You can only gain marks if the examiner can read your script.

Keep your answer simple and to the point. It should have clear explanations of your reasoning. Even when working quickly, keep your eye on the task. You must answer the specific question that has been set.

Don't be tempted to waffle. Remember that time taken to write irrelevant material is time lost from another question. Don't waste time including irrelevant facts just because you memorised them during revision. This may do you more harm than good.

 And now . . .

15.1 **Prepare at an early stage.** Even before your thoughts turn to revision, look through the course handbook and other information to make sure you have a good idea of how the material presented will be assessed. This will help keep your note-taking and reading strategies in tune with your exam strategy.

15.2 **Create a strategy for each of your exams.** Discuss your strategy with someone else on the course to see what they think of it and how they intend to handle the exam.

15.3 **Ask a tutor's advice.** If you are in doubt about any of the assumptions that may lie behind your strategy, then ask a tutor.

Improving your exam performance

How to avoid common pitfalls

Why aren't you doing as well as you'd like to in your exams and tests? This chapter focusses on the main reasons why exam answers are marked down and provides a framework for assessing how you could improve.

Key topics:

→ Identifying reasons for weak performance and areas for improvement
→ How to ensure you answer the question
→ Reviewing your answers to gain marks

Key terms
Brainstorm   Question-spotting   Value judgement

Poor exam performance is a relative term that depends on your expectations. There will probably be occasions when you can easily diagnose the reasons for weak marks. Lack of preparation, poor performance in the exam room, or revising the 'wrong' topics are common examples. In these instances, your expectations after the exam were probably low and you can accept that you deserved a low grade.

At other times, you may feel your marks were not as good as you thought they were going to be. You may have misunderstood the topic or failed to understand all the nuances of the question. Here, there is a gap between your expectation and the results of your efforts – one that is vitally important to understand if you wish to do better in future.

Table 16.1 Checklist of possible reasons for poor exam marks. Use the list to find routes for improving your performance.

Reason	Possible cure(s)
Not answering the exact question as set: • failing to recognise the specialist terms • failing to carry out the precise instruction • failing to address all aspects	A range of solutions – discussed in detail within this chapter
Poor time management: • failing to match the extent of the answer(s) to the time allocated • spending too long on one question and not enough on the others	A better exam strategy is required (Ch 15)
Failing to weight parts of the answer appropriately: not recognising that one aspect (perhaps involving more complex ideas) may carry more marks than another	A better essay plan may be required (Ch 19)
Failing to provide evidence to support an answer: not including examples or not stating basic facts or definitions	Need to realise this material is required to gain marks (p. 172). A better essay plan may be required
Failing to illustrate an answer appropriately: • not including a relevant diagram • providing a diagram that does not aid communication	Need to understand how diagrams should be used to support writing (Ch 12)
Incomplete or shallow answers: • failing to answer appropriately due to lack of knowledge • not considering the topic in sufficient depth	Need a better revision plan (Ch 8), a better revision technique (Ch 11) or a better understanding of the thinking process demanded at university (Ch 1)
Providing irrelevant evidence to support an answer: 'waffling' to fill space	See material on answering the question (Ch 18)
Illegible handwriting: if it can't be read, it can't be marked	May need to slow down writing speed or change writing style
Poor English: facts and ideas are not expressed clearly	Need to address academic writing skills
Lack of logic or structure to the answer	Need to plan your writing better (Ch 15, Ch 19)
Factual errors	Poor note-taking, learning, revision or recall (Ch 1, Ch 11, Ch 12)
Failing to correct obvious mistakes	Need to review and proof-read answers (Ch 15, p. 148)

→ Identifying reasons for weak performance and areas for improvement

Where might you have gone wrong in the past, and how might you improve? To find out, you will need to:

- **Reflect carefully on past exams.** Look back and think about how things went, and whether you might have been guilty of any of faults shown in Tables 15.1 and 16.1. You may find it beneficial to look at the original question papers to jog your memory. Also, refer to any feedback on coursework or comments on exam scripts if these are available to you (Ch 10). If you don't understand any of the comments, then try to meet with the marker and ask for an explanation. Such discussions can often be very valuable, so it is worth making the effort required.

- **Try to do something about the faults you have identified.** Many of the causes of poor exam performance are simple to correct, once you have identified which might apply to you. If, after reading through this 'self-help' chapter, you still do not understand where you went wrong or what corrective action to take, you should ask to meet with your tutor(s) to seek their advice.

→ How to ensure you answer the question

Most lecturers agree that the number one reason for a well-prepared student losing marks is because their answers *do not address the question*. This is especially true for essay-style questions but also true for short-answer questions and other assignments.

The main tips for answering questions directly and purposefully include:

- Ensuring your work is well planned.
- Making sure you consider all aspects of the question.
- Explaining what *you* understand by the question.
- Focussing on the precise task you have been asked to do.
- Keeping to the point.
- Making sure you answer all elements in multi-part questions.
- Avoiding making value judgements.

Examples of solutions to poor performance

If you ran out of time and some of your answers were incomplete, then you probably need a better strategy for using time in your exams (Ch 15). This is a simple fault to rectify.

If you feel that your vocabulary is weak or your English style inappropriate, then you might need a longer-term approach that would involve creating a glossary or reading about text structuring or punctuation (Ch 18).

Include basic material in your answer, such as key terms and their definitions, and critical dates and names. Especially if a strict marking scheme is being used, tutors will be unable to award you marks if you do not provide this information. Draw on your understanding of the whole topic when creating your answer plan. Don't just focus on key phrases of the question in isolation, but consider their context. Be aware of the risk, if you have misguidedly decided to 'question-spot' (Ch 9), of answering your own pre-prepared question, rather than the one that has actually been set.

Reasons for loss of marks at advanced levels

The following are reasons why you might be marked down at higher levels of study:

- Not providing enough in-depth information.
- Providing a descriptive rather than an analytical answer - focussing on facts, rather than deeper aspects of a topic.
- Not thinking critically about a topic - or, more likely, not providing the evidence of your deeper-level thoughts.
- Not setting a problem in context, or not demonstrating a wider understanding of the topic. However, make sure you don't overdo this, or you may risk not answering the question set.
- Not giving enough evidence of reading around the subject. This can be corrected by quoting relevant papers and reviews.
- Not considering both sides of a topic/debate, or not arriving at a conclusion if you have done so.

→ Reviewing your answers to gain marks

Many students want to get out of the exam room as soon as possible, but you should not do this unless you are convinced you have squeezed every last mark out of the paper. Your exam strategy (**Ch 15**) should always include an allocation of time for reviewing. Correcting simple errors could mean the difference between a pass or a fail or between degree classifications. These are some of the things you could look for when reviewing your work:

- **Basics.** Make sure you have numbered your answers, answered the right number of questions, and have complied with the instructions in the rubric at the start of the paper.

- **Spelling, grammar and sense.** Read through the answer critically (try to imagine it has been written by someone else) and correct any obvious errors that strike you. Does the text make sense? Do the sentences and paragraphs flow smoothly?

- **Structure and relevance.** Once again, ask yourself whether you have really answered the question that was set. Have you followed precisely the instruction(s) in the title? Is anything missed out? Are the different parts linked together well? Look for inconsistencies in argument. Add new material if necessary.

'Small-scale' corrections like spelling errors and changes to punctuation marks can be made directly in your text using standard proof-reading symbols if required. If you want to add text because you find you have missed something out, place an insert mark ($\wedge$ or λ) in the text and/or margin, with the annotation 'see additional paragraph x'; then write this paragraph, clearly identified, at the end of the answer. You will not lose any marks for having to do this; indeed, you will probably gain some.

---

smart tip

Try to help staff to help you

It's important to realise that the person who marks your work is not an adversary. Most lecturers are disappointed when giving students a poor grade, but they approach the marking process professionally and with ruthless objectivity. Tutors are often very frustrated when they see that simple changes in approach might have led to a better mark, and they cannot assume that you know things that you do not put down on paper.

Practical tips for improving your exam performance

Go in well prepared. Of course, you'd expect any lecturer to say this, because in terms of gaining good marks, there is no substitute for effective revision. However, being well prepared means more than memorising facts and concepts. To do well you also need to arrive at the exam room in a good mental state, with a strategy (Ch 14), a positive attitude and the determination to get down to work quickly and effectively.

Assess question options efficiently. If you have a choice, do not dwell on your decision. Give each question a quick appraisal and allocate a notional 'grade' to it (for example, a mark out of 10); then get started on an answer that you think will be relatively straightforward.

Convert your initial thoughts into a plan as quickly as possible. You can do this very quickly simply by numbering the headings in the brainstorm in the order you intend to write about them.

Think in the same way as the examiner will be thinking. What would you look for in an answer to the question? How would you allocate the marks to each facet of the answer? This deceptively simple approach helps you to plan answers better and improve the depth of your approach to the question.

Make sure you are responding at the right level. Have a look at Table 1.1 and p. 172, and consider the definitions of 'higher-level' thought processes. Perhaps you are not providing enough evidence of analytical thought, synthesis or evaluation in your answers. Think about topics with these notions in mind and relate the different thought processes to the learning objectives you have been given.

Make 'Am I answering the question?' your mantra. Repeat this time and time again during your exams. Ask yourself this as you plan answers, as you write the text, and as you review what you have written.

And now . . .

16.1 Analyse your past exam performances. Work through the points in Table 16.1 and make a resolution to improve at least one aspect of your revision or exam technique.

16.2 Think about timetabling. If you acknowledge that the main reason for a previous weak performance was lack of organised effort, consider whether you might benefit from creating (and sticking to) a more structured revision timetable (**Ch 7**).

16.3 Think more deeply about your subject. If feedback suggests that the depth of your answers is too shallow, but you don't fully understand how you could improve, have a look at the material on thinking processes (**Ch 1**) to see whether this might make things clearer.

Tackling specific types of exam and assessment

Multiple-choice and short-answer questions

How to tackle short-answer formats

Many university exams, especially at early stages, test your knowledge using 'objective' question types, which tend to be short and demand factual answers. This chapter explains how to adjust your revision and exam technique to suit these forms of assessment.

Key topics:

→ Tackling multiple-choice questions
→ Dealing with short-answer questions
→ Advice for other types of short-form question

Key terms
Distractor   Formative assessment   Multiple-choice question (MCQ)
Negative marking   Short-answer question (SAQ)

A multiple-choice question (MCQ) is one in which you are presented with alternative answers and asked to select one that is correct. In some cases, you may be asked to identify several correct answers rather than one. A short-answer question (SAQ) deals with topics of limited scope and you are generally expected to produce a mini-essay, bulleted points or a diagram in response.

Both MCQs and SAQs are used as alternatives to standard essay questions as a means of testing the breadth and detail of your knowledge across the whole syllabus. Generally, they are mixed with other forms of questions that are better for testing the depth of your knowledge and analytical capabilities.

Good technique and strategy with MCQs and SAQs can improve your marks and save time for answering other questions.

The most common form of MCQ provides some statement or question, then offers four possible answers. One of the answers is correct and the other three are known as distractors.

● If the question simply seeks a factual answer, such as the date something happened, or the name of a person, then the answers may simply present a series of alternatives to the true answer.

● Sometimes the question is devised to test your knowledge of technical terms or jargon, in which case the distractors may use similar-sounding terms to the correct answer.

● Some questions involve a quantitative problem and then give possible answers that you can only arrive at by doing the requisite calculation. The answers provided may include values that you will obtain if you carry out a faulty calculation.

There may be a special way of identifying the answer, such as shading in a box or selecting an option with your mouse. Read the rubric carefully to make sure you do the right thing.

Increasingly, MCQs are presented via computers. This is usually termed computer-aided assessment (CAA) or online assessment (OA). Use of CAA means that the answers can be 'instantly' checked. Where such systems are used for formative assessments that are not part of your final assessment, the software may allow you to receive feedback on incorrect answers to help you learn more about aspects you evidently did not understand.

Example MCQ

The bone at the front of the leg below the knee is called:

A The fibula

B The tibia

C The femur

D The cruciate

B is the correct answer; A, C and D are distractors. You may know that all the potential answers are parts of a leg, but unless you know the anatomy well, you may not be able to identify the correct answer.

A good method for approaching MCQ papers is as follows:

- **First sweep.** Read through the questions fairly rapidly, noting the 'correct' answer in those you can attempt immediately, perhaps on a separate sheet. Don't fill in or submit any answers properly yet.

- **Second sweep.** Go through the paper again, checking your original answers, and thinking for a longer time about uncertain answers. This time, mark up the answer sheet properly or submit answers online. Leave questions you are still uncertain about at this stage.

- **Third sweep.** Now tackle the difficult questions and those that require longer to answer (for example, those based on numerical problems). At this stage, whether you should guess answers depends on the marking regime being used (see 'Optimising marks' in the Practical tips section below).

One reason for adopting this three-phase approach is that considering the full set of questions may prompt you to recall facts relevant to difficult questions. You can also spend more time per question on the difficult ones.

---

smart tip

Getting used to software

If you are offered the option to practise CAA/OA, take it. Familiarity with the software may save you time in the real exam.

→ Dealing with short-answer questions

The various styles that can be encompassed within the SAQ format (see below) allow for more demanding questions than MCQs. For this form of question, few if any marks are given for writing style. Answers are often expected in note form or as a diagram. Think in 'bulletpoint' mode and list the crucial points only. The time for answering SAQ questions may be tight, so get down to work fast, starting with answers that demand remembered facts.

In SAQ papers, there is often a choice of questions. Choose carefully – it may be better to gain half marks for a correct answer to half a question than to provide a largely irrelevant answer or one that seems to cover the whole topic, but does so too superficially. Consider all sections of the question before you start answering, in case you cannot cope with secondary questions.

Always answer the question as requested – this is true for all questions, but especially important for SAQs. If the question asks for a diagram, make sure you provide one, and label it well; if it asks for *n* aspects of a topic, try to list this number of points; if there are two or more parts, provide appropriate answers to all aspects. This may seem obvious, but many marks are lost for not following instructions. Bear in mind that markers may award marks for correct use of key phrases – so try to use the terms and subject jargon normally used in the resources, lectures and discussions. Finally, remember to check through your answers at the end. You'll be able to correct obvious mistakes and possibly add points that come to mind when rereading.

→ Advice for other types of short-form question

- **Multiple-response questions.** These are essentially MCQs in which more than one answer can be correct – and you may or may not be told how many. Marks are usually awarded for having the correct combination of answers, so you will really have to know the topic well to score highly. Guessing is not advised, especially if you do not know how many answers are correct.

- **Fill-in-the-missing-word questions.** These can be tough options because you are not given prompts for the correct answer. However, you may be able to obtain clues from the surrounding text or other questions. When marked by software, allowance is often made for common misspellings, but it's worth taking special care over spelling in such cases: there is no guarantee that 'your' misspelling will be included and there may be no human check on the wrong answers.

- **'Matching' questions.** These present you with a series of options and ask you to link these to a series of answers or matching phrases. Start with the easy matches and see which questions and options remain. If you need to guess, remember that one incorrect answer will actually result in two lost marks, because you will have ruled out the correct answer to another question.

- **'Hot-spot' and other pictorial question formats.** These mainly apply to online assessment; the question may ask that you identify part of a diagram using the cursor – perhaps by clicking, dragging an arrow or symbol, or by dragging images to the correct spot. Alternatively, you may be asked to provide text for a labelled item. Do not rush such questions: make sure you are especially careful to identify the exact location where markers should be placed.

Gobbets, précis and other specialised assessments

Because of their subject-specific nature, it is not possible to give generalised advice on these. Consult the course handbook or lecturers to find out the recommended structure and content and the best way to approach them in exams.

Practical tips for addressing MCQs and SAQs

Revise appropriately. If your paper includes MCQs or SAQs, keep this in mind as you study. Think how material might be assessed in these ways and make sure you learn potentially examinable definitions and facts. Also make sure you can draw and label relevant diagrams. You may find it useful to discuss potential questions with fellow class members.

Take a logical approach to MCQs. When unsure of an answer, the first stage is to rule out options that are clearly absurd or have obviously been placed there to distract you. Next, looking at the remaining options, can you judge between contrasting pairs with alternative answers? Logically, both cannot be correct, so you should see if you can rule one of the pair out. Watch out, however, in case *both* may be irrelevant to the answer.

Write down key information before looking at MCQ options. If you have key dates, facts or formulae to remember, write these down as soon as the exam starts. If you do this before looking at the options in the exam questions, you will be less likely to be confused or distracted by similar-sounding options.

Hints for numerical questions. If an MCQ involves a calculation, try to do this independently from the answers, so you are not influenced by them. Assuming you have done the appropriate revision, and have the required knowledge and skills, numerical questions in SAQ papers can be a valuable means of accumulating marks, because it is possible to score 100 per cent in them if your answer is correct and laid out appropriately.

Optimising marks. The best way of tackling MCQs depends on the marking regime. If there is a penalty for incorrect answers in a multiple-choice test (often referred to as 'negative marking'), the best strategy is *not* to answer questions when you know your answer is a guess. Depending on the penalty, it may be beneficial to guess, if you can narrow the choice down to two options, but beware false or irrelevant alternatives. If there are no such penalties, then you should provide an answer to all questions in the paper, even if this means guessing in some cases.

Guessing. If you have to do this to complete the paper (assuming negative marking doesn't apply), go with your first hunch for the answer rather than a second thought that might be influenced by the distractors. Your subconscious may have arrived at the correct answer, without your conscious mind understanding why.

17.1 Compensate for any lack of past MCQ papers.
Departments are usually reluctant to release past papers for
MCQs, since there will often be only a limited pool of good
discriminatory questions. Staff also fear that students will simply
memorise answers to the questions in the pool, rather than
learning the whole course. You can compensate for this by
making up your own MCQs as part of your revision - this is
a good way of understanding the examiner's likely frame of
mind and of spotting topics to revise and facts to memorise.
If studying as a group, you could all submit a specified number
of questions and then answer each other's.

17.2 Seek out model answers to SAQs. These may be provided
in course handbooks. They will give you an idea of the length and
depth of answer required in your subject, as well as the general
style of question.

17.3 Think through your exam strategy. MCQs and SAQs often
form elements of composite exam papers involving several
sections, each being made up of questions of a particular type.
Time management in these papers can be difficult because of this
complexity, so think through the order in which you will tackle
the parts and how much time you should devote to each MCQ
sweep and SAQ question. Because time is often limited in SAQ
papers, it is particularly important to share out time so that you
don't leave any questions unanswered.

18 | Numerical questions

How to approach quantitative problems

It's worth paying close attention to mathematical aspects of your course because, in exam situations, if you get the answers right, it is possible to obtain very high marks. Even if you don't consider yourself particularly numerate, tackling these topics head-on can repay the effort.

Key topics:

→ Why do examiners ask numerical questions?
→ Learning key mathematical skills
→ Why practice is essential
→ Tackling the problem

Key terms
Dimensional analysis   Numeracy   Part-marking   Quantitative

Some students favour questions that require a numerical or statistical approach. Others struggle where maths is involved, or suffer from a lack of preparation. Whichever category applies to you, it is worth the effort of conquering mathematical assessments, because the payback can be excellent – answering this type of question correctly is one of the few ways in which you can obtain 100 per cent in a university exam.

→ Why do examiners ask numerical questions?

Numerical (quantitative) problems allow examiners to test the following:

● your numeracy, mathematical skills and problem-solving abilities;
● your capacity to recall, understand and apply theoretical models within 'real-life' scenarios;
● your ability to think clearly and work quickly under pressure;

- your ability to follow a standard format for calculation, particularly where it may be related to professional competence, as in Engineering and Accountancy;
- your ability to present a logical sequence of operations clearly, such that another person can understand what you have done.

→ Learning key mathematical skills

You won't get very far without knowing the basic maths required for the types of problems you will encounter. This should be easy to find out by consulting the course handbook, examining past papers, reading textbooks or by speaking to lecturers or tutors. If you feel that your numeracy skills are 'rusty' in particular areas, make sure that you consult appropriate texts and revise the principles and techniques involved, as this effort will be amply rewarded. If your course requires more advanced mathematics, then it is likely that specialist modules or other forms of assistance will be available to you.

→ Why practice is essential

When it comes to numerical problems, there is simply no substitute for practice. If you have a block about numerical work, practice at problem-solving or standard forms of analysis will:

- demystify the procedures involved, which, in reality, may only involve elementary mathematical operations and just appear complex on the surface;
- allow you to gain confidence, so that you don't panic when confronted with an unfamiliar or apparently complex form of problem;
- help you work faster, because the pattern of work will have become routine;

- help you to recognise the various forms a problem can take. This is useful because there are a limited number of ways lecturers can present questions and it is important to identify the relevant formulae or approach to adopt as soon as possible;
- help imprint the standard form of analysis and presentation, ensuring that you automatically adopt the correct procedure and presentation style.

smart tip

Revision tips for numerical questions

Try as many examples from past papers and problem sheets as you can. A useful tactic is to invent your own problems, as this helps you understand the equations and mathematical models better.

→ Tackling the problem

A step-by-step approach is recommended. This may not always be the fastest method, but mistakes often occur when students miss out stages of a calculation, combine simple calculations, or do not make what they have done obvious to themselves or the examiner. Error tracing (and, importantly, part-marking) is easier when all stages in a calculation are laid out sequentially.

Part-marking

This is where the examiner will give marks for the steps of a calculation even though the final result is incorrect due to a mathematical or copying error at some early stage. Part marks can only be given if the stages in a calculation are laid out clearly. Therefore, if you know you have ended up with an incorrect answer, perhaps because the scale of it is absurd, do not immediately scribble all over your working. Move on to another question and return to the earlier one at the end of the exam; even if you can't spot the error, you may receive part marks.

Approach the problem thoughtfully

If presented as a story or scenario, you may need to 'decode' the problem to decide which equations or rules need to be applied.

- Read the problem carefully – the text may give clues as to how it should be tackled. Be certain of what is required as an answer before starting.

- Analyse what kind of problem it is. Which equation(s) or approach will be applicable? If this is not obvious, consider the dimensions/units of the information available and think how they could be fitted to a relevant formula or form of analysis. In formula-based questions, a favourite trick of examiners is to make you rearrange a familiar equation before you can work out the answer. Another is to make you use two or more equations in series. You may therefore need to revise the rules for rearranging formulae.

- Check that you have, or can derive, all the information required. It is unusual, but not unknown, for examiners to supply redundant information. So, if you decide not to use some of the information given, be confident about why you do not require it.

- Decide on the format and units in which to present the answer. This is sometimes suggested to you. If the problem requires many changes in the prefixes to units, it may be a good idea to convert all data to base SI units at the outset.

- If a problem appears complex, break it down into component parts.

Present your answer clearly

The way you present your answer obviously needs to fit the individual problem. In general, the final answer should be presented as a meaningful statement and any number given should carry appropriate significant figures and units. You should always show your working – most markers will only penalise a mistake once if the remaining operations are performed correctly, but they can only do this if you make those operations visible.

Guidelines for presenting an answer include:

- Where appropriate, make your assumptions explicit – most mathematical models require that certain criteria are met before they can be legitimately applied, and some involve assumptions and approximations. In some cases you may be given credit for stating these clearly at the outset.
- Outline your strategy for answering briefly, perhaps explaining the applicable formula or definitions that suit the approach to be taken. Give details of what the symbols mean (and their units) at this point. If rearranging a formula, show how you have done this, using symbols first, then substituting relevant numerical values.
- Convert to the desired units step by step, that is, taking each variable in turn. Try to get into the habit of writing all numbers with their units, unless they are truly dimensionless.

smart tip

Presentation tips

When you have obtained a numerical answer in the desired units, rewrite this in meaningful English and <u>underline the answer</u>. Make sure you use an appropriate number of significant figures.

Check your answer

Having written out your answer, you should check it methodically:

- Is the answer of the magnitude you might reasonably expect? You should be alerted to an error if an answer is absurdly large or small. If using a calculator, beware of absurd results that could arise from faulty key-pressing or logic. Double-check any result obviously standing out from others in a series.
- Do the units make sense and match up with the answer required?
- Do you get the same answer if you recalculate using a different method?

smart tip

What if you know your answer is wrong?

Be prepared to say that you know your answer is wrong, but cannot identify where the error has come – you may get a small amount of credit for showing this awareness. Also, if you know what to do to obtain an answer, but not *how* to do it, you may gain some credit for giving as much detail as you can.

Practical tips for approaching numerical questions in exams

Check your calculator. Before your exam date, ensure that you are allowed to use a calculator, and confirm that it is a model that is permitted for use if there are any restrictions. Make sure you understand how to carry out relevant functions. If your calculator is battery-operated, ensure a fresh one is fitted or take a spare.

Analyse the question type. Make sure you understand which formula or formulae to use, or which approach to attempt before starting.

Work methodically and carefully. Double-check each step. Write neatly and add vital information such as units or assumptions.

Pay attention to presentation. Follow the tips given earlier in this chapter and always provide units or a written explanation with the answer.

Never give up. Even if you think you can't complete the answer, don't give up. Try to do the basics or a part answer, perhaps noting any points you can recall in a list. The part marks obtained could make the difference between a pass and a fail.

GO And now . . .

18.1 When revising, create a page of formulae relevant to your subject. Note situations where each is normally applied.

18.2 Try to categorise types of numerical questions that have been asked in past exam papers. For example, work out which formulae should be applied and how they may be rearranged or linked. Thinking at this level will help you identify how to approach questions more rapidly and with more confidence.

18.3 Practise! This really is the key to success where numerical problems are concerned.

How to maximise your marks

The essay is a traditional method of university assessment that allows you to discuss concepts and issues in depth. It also allows you flexibility in the way you compose your answer, and in exam situations you'll need to decide this quickly. This chapter focusses on approaches you can take to deciding on content, organising this and producing an effective answer.

Key topics:

→ What lecturers are looking for in essay answers
→ Planning essay answers in exams
→ The importance of addressing the question
→ Reviewing your answers

Key terms
Critical thinking   Formative assessment   Instruction words
Personal pronoun   Value judgement

Developing your writing skills is a gradual process, and one that is best done with time at your disposal. In most exams you will not be able to spend a long time on constructing your response to the set task, and will be expected to perform under time pressure, without aids like dictionaries and thesauri and with very limited scope to review, edit and rewrite. This chapter provides tips for writing essay-style answers quickly and effectively so you can maximise the marks you obtain.

→ What lecturers are looking for in essay answers

Essay-style questions are mainly used by tutors to elicit an in-depth answer to a complex issue. Other shorter forms tend to be included when they want you to address knowledge over a wide area, whereas the essay format allows you to develop an argument, explain alternative views or provide a high level of detail in your answer. Because you cannot be expected to know all topics in this sort of depth, there is often an element of choice in essay exam papers.

Critical thinking

Essays are commonly used when tutors expect you to think more deeply. Often what you have to do is not framed as a question but as an instruction. Typically, you will be expected to:

- **apply** knowledge and understanding;
- **analyse** information;
- **synthesise** new ideas or treatments of facts;
- **evaluate** issues, positions and arguments.

See Table 1.1 (p. 6) for further explanation of what's expected under these headings, and watch out for instruction words that invite these approaches.

→ Planning essay answers in exams

The main advice is to keep your writing simple. Working quickly, use a spider diagram or mind map to generate ideas relevant to the question. From this, decide on an outline structure. This approach helps you to think laterally as well as in a linear manner - important so that you generate all the points relevant to your answer. You should probably think in terms of three basic components:

- **The introduction:** sets the context, gives an insight as to how you intend to approach the topic and states briefly what your answer will say.
- **The main body:** presents the information, the argument or key points of your response.
- **The conclusion:** sums up the answer as stated, reinforces the position outlined in the introduction, and puts the whole answer into a wider context.

Introductions compared with conclusions

- The **introduction** outlines the topic and your aim in general terms, while the conclusion states your argument, viewpoint or findings supported by the evidence and information you have discussed in the main body.

- The terminology used in the **conclusion** is more specialised, because it will have been introduced and explained in the main body of the work as a means of expressing ideas more succinctly and knowledgeably.

An important way in which marks can be lost is through poor structuring of exam answers (**Ch 16**). Ideally, your outline plan will lead to an obvious structure for the main body of the text, but often in exam situations, an essay evolves once you begin to write. This is because the act of writing stimulates development of thought, potentially leading to changes in order and in content. In these cases, your initial outline plan should be seen as a flexible guideline that may change as you begin to think more deeply about the topic.

Writer's block

If you find you tend to get stuck at the start of an essay answer, try starting with a definition or simple statement of fact.

On the other hand, if the planning phase is ignored completely, and you only think about the structure while you write, then you can end up with a weakly structured essay. Table 19.1 describes some common pitfalls that can occur when students fail to consider the structure of their writing.

Quotations and citations in exam answers

Do not become bogged down in trying to remember direct quotes word for word (possible exceptions are in literature and law exams). Just give the sense of the quote, its relevance to your answer and its source.

Table 19.1 **Common faults in the structure of essay-style answers.** In most of these examples, paying more attention to the planning phase will result in a better structure, and, hence, better marks.

Symptom of weakness in structure	Analysis of the problem
The magical mystery tour. This type of answer rambles on, drifting from point to disconnected point with no real structure.	The essay may contain valuable content, but marks will be lost because this is not organised and parts are not connected appropriately to create a coherent response.
No introduction and/or no conclusion. The main body contains many useful points, but fails to introduce them and fails to draw conclusions based on them.	Facts, concepts and ideas alone are not enough – evidence must be provided of deeper-level analytical thinking. The introduction and conclusions are important parts where this can be achieved.
The overly-detailed answer. The main body of the answer contains a wealth of information, some of which is relevant and some not. Despite the finely-grained detail, little structure is evident and there is no discrimination between the important and the unimportant.	The writer has probably been preoccupied with showing how much has been memorised, without showing how much has been understood. Relevance of the material in relation to the instruction given has not been considered at the planning stage, or as the essay-writing progresses.
The stream of consciousness. Often written as if it were a conversational monologue, this lacks internal organisation, few (or too many) signposting words, no (or few) paragraphs, and little apparent logic.	Academic writing style involves structural as well as linguistic components. Both are important elements of a good answer. Hence, the writing needs to guide the reader along a logical path to enable understanding.
The waffly, irrelevant answer. Unfocussed, fails to get to grips with the question and may contain large amounts of irrelevant information, offered up seemingly without regard for the topic set.	Greater attention needs to be paid to analysis of the instruction given and converting these thoughts into a coherent answer plan. Irrelevant material should not be used as it will gain no marks.
The half-an-answer. Fails to appreciate that there were two (or more) parts to the question. Focusses solely on the first part.	The essay should cover all aspects of the question as more marks may be allocated to the secondary part(s). This should be reflected in the essay plan and eventual structure.
Structure dominated by quotes. This might start with a hackneyed quote or be interspersed with extensive memorised quotes, with little effective use of these.	This type of structure leaves little room for evidence of original thought. Few marks are given for having a good memory – it's what is done with the information that counts.

→ The importance of addressing the question

Another important way in which marks can be lost is when answers do not address the question (see **Ch 16**). You can avoid this by:

- Making sure you consider all aspects of the question. Brainstorming techniques can help you achieve this.

- Explaining what *you* understand by the question (perhaps in the introductory paragraph). This will make you think about the question and may clear up any doubt about how it can be interpreted. However, make sure you do not narrow the topic beyond what would be reasonable.

- Focussing on the precise task you have been asked to do. Remember to tackle the question actually asked and not the one you would have liked to answer – this is a risk in question-spotting.

- Ensuring your answer is planned. Creating a plan will make you think about relevance and the logic of your argument.

- Keeping to the point. Including irrelevant or repetitive content will not gain you any marks and the time you spend writing it will be wasted, stopping you from gaining marks on other questions. Having said that, no marks are given for 'white space': even a few general points of principle may result in enough marks to help you pass, when added to those gained in other, better, answers.

- Making sure you answer all parts in multi-part questions. These may not be worded in two or more sentences: phrases such as 'compare and contrast' and 'cause and effect' should alert you to this. Make sure that the weighting in marks given to questions is reflected in the length of the component parts of your answer.

- Avoiding making unsupported value judgements. These are statements of the writer's views, often using subjective language, and which fail to provide sound evidence to support the position put forward. Make sure you write objectively and avoid using the personal pronouns 'I', 'you', 'we' and 'one'.

Mixing topics

Sometimes examination questions will blend two topics so that you may find that you can only answer half the question. This is one of the dangers of question-spotting (**Ch 9**).

Analysing the wording of each question

This requires a bit more than simply thinking about *what* you are being asked to do. You need to take a broader and more in-depth look at the task in the context of the whole question. To do this, you must consider:

- **The instruction word.** In what category does that place the task? For example, have you been asked to act, describe, analyse, argue, or do something else completely?
- **The topic.** What is the core topic about?
- **The aspect(s) to be covered.** What particular aspect of the topic has to be considered?
- **Any restriction(s).** What limits have been imposed on the discussion?

Your answer must encompass each element of the task to ensure that it is a logical response to the task you were set. What you write must be relevant. Superfluous material or digressions will not earn you marks.

→ Reviewing your answers

This is an essential stage of creating a sound piece of academicwriting, whether for an in-course assignment or exam. Tips for reviewing essay answers in an exam situation are provided in **Ch 16**.

Practical tips for boosting your essay marks

Have potential answer formats in mind as you go into an exam. Ideally, your revision and pre-exam preparation will have given you a good idea of the exam format and even potential exam questions. This will ensure you do not have to start answers completely from scratch.

Use notes and plans effectively. It is perfectly acceptable practice to make notes in exam books; however, you should always score through them before you submit the answer paper. A single diagonal line will suffice. Sometimes your plan may be used by the examiner to cross-check details of your answer (but do not count on this).

Keep your writing simple. If you are to stick to your exam strategy, you must not lose valuable time creating an attention-grabbing piece of writing. You won't have time or space to refine your answer in the same way as you would with a piece of coursework. In particular, don't labour the introduction with fine phrases – get straight to the point of the question and give your response to it.

Balance your effort appropriately. For example, in exam answers your introduction need not be overly long. Most marks will be awarded for the main body and conclusions, so spend more time and brainpower on them.

Focus on providing evidence of deeper thinking. Especially at higher levels of study, this will help you gain better grades. On the assumption that you are able to include *basic* information and display an understanding of it, you can gain marks for:

- supplying additional and relevant detail at the expected depth;
- providing an analytical answer rather than a descriptive one – focussing on deeper aspects of a topic, rather than merely recounting facts;
- setting a problem in context, and demonstrating a wider understanding of the topic; however, make sure you don't overdo this, or you may risk not answering the question set – remember that you cannot be expected to give the same amount of detail in an exam answer as you would in a piece of essay-style coursework;
- giving enough evidence of reading around the subject, by quoting relevant papers and reviews and mentioning author names and dates of publication;
- considering all sides of a topic/debate, and arriving at a clear conclusion – you may have to take into account *and explain* two or more viewpoints, and possibly weigh them up, according to the question set; where appropriate, your answer should demonstrate that you realise that the issue is complex and possibly unresolved.

Make sure you aren't losing marks due to poor presentation. Despite the time pressure, exam answers need to be legible and clearly laid out. If feedback indicates that tutors are having problems in reading your work, or consider it untidy, paying attention to this could be an easy way of gaining marks.

GO And now . . .

19.1 Review essay-style questions in past exam papers.
Look at these particularly from the point of view of the *depth*
of answers required. Consider both the instruction word used
and the context to gain an appreciation of the level of thinking
demanded.

**19.2 Focus on definitions and possible formats during
revision.** If you have trouble getting your answers started
during exams, it can be a useful device to start with a definition;
alternatively, think about stating the situation, the problem and
then the potential solution. This might not be applicable to all
scenarios, but if you are really stuck this will at least give you a
framework for thinking and writing.

**19.3 Use formative assessment exercises to improve your
English.** If you recognise that your use of language is weak, then
take advantage of all formative assessment exercises to help
you improve. Speak with markers and tutors about how you
might enhance your marks. You may find that analysing writing
technique can help, especially if you are aware of specific
weaknesses, such as punctuation or structuring.

20 | Tutorial assessment

How to make your contribution count

This chapter explains what is expected of you in a tutorial and what might be taken into consideration when tutors or peers assess your engagement with the topic or problem.

Key topics:
→ Engaging fully with the topic
→ Criteria for assessment of tutorial participation

Key terms
Assessment criteria   Marking scheme   Tutorial

The main purpose of a university tutorial is to learn interactively with others, either through discussion and debate of issues, or by considering problems you have been asked to address. Your output, such as a related essay or the answers to numerical questions, may be assessed, and, in some cases, your role as a participant may be evaluated. You need to understand exactly what is going to be considered so that you can make your contribution count.

→ Engaging fully with the topic

Preparation for tutorials is essential. You will gain more from these meetings if you are well prepared. However, in the context of assessment you need to think in greater detail about how you go about tackling a set of problems or a topic. This will differ slightly depending on the type of tutorial.

Problem-solving tutorials

For problem-solving tutorials, you may be asked to work through problems beforehand or, conversely, you may be asked to review the problems in preparation for working through them as a group in the tutorial.

The best approach for this type of tutorial is to:

- Identify the area or theme being addressed.
- Read over the relevant sections in your textbook and lecture notes.
- Equip yourself with the skills to do the task. This might mean revising an area of maths or understanding relevant formulae.
- Look over the examples to see whether they are all of similar difficulty or whether they are ranged in ascending difficulty. This could be a deliberate way of leading you through the process of developing a proof for a formula and then applying it to a more complex problem.

Discussion-based tutorials

For discussion-based tutorials, the topic will generally be given in advance.

- Analyse the topic in the same way that you would analyse a topic for a written assignment.
- Read over the relevant sections in your lecture notes and do the prescribed reading. Who are the key commentators on the topic? What are their perspectives on the topic?
- Make notes of key ideas and principles as appropriate, so that you can refer to these in the tutorials.
- You should be looking for aspects such as:
  - for and against positions;
  - cause-and-effect scenarios;
  - comparison of similar circumstances or attitudes;
  - contrasting viewpoints and the evidence in support and refutation;
  - inconsistencies and flaws in argument;
  - parallels and analogies used to illustrate points.

> **smart tip**
>
> **Presence and participation**
>
> Slipping into a lecture 10 minutes after the start may go unnoticed. The same will not be true of a late arrival in a tutorial. Show courtesy to your fellow students and the tutor by being on time and engaging actively with the intensive work designed to develop your understanding of the tutorial theme.

Relationships between tutorials and exams

Exams are not simply based on the lectures. They draw from the extended reading, exercises and tutorials that form part of your personal study. It is worth looking carefully at tutorial topics and the preparatory work associated with them when you are planning your revision. Be sure to include these topics as part of the work to be covered in your preparation for exam-based assessment.

→ Criteria for assessment of tutorial participation

Tutorial assessment may count for between 5 and 25 per cent of your total course assessment, with part or all of that mark being for 'participation', depending on the subject. Check the course handbook for details. Several generic aspects may be taken into account:

- your attendance over the series of tutorials;
- your active participation in the discussion or problem-solving aspects of the tutorial;
- evidence of reading and/or other preparation;
- your ability to think analytically and critically about points raised during the tutorial;
- your ability to present and defend a viewpoint, and the quality of your counter-arguments;
- your ability to relate the tutorial activity to other parts of the course and to the wider subject area;
- your ability to interact considerately and constructively with others.

Student-led tutorials

Sometimes tutorials are organised so that each student is given an opportunity to lead the tutorial discussion, while the tutor observes the interplay of argument and debate. If you are required to participate in tutorials in this way, then the strategies you adopt to deal with comments of the other group members will be important.

Practical tips for tutorial assessment

For problem-solving tutorials:

Consider how the marks awarded for each tutorial will affect your assessment. Find out how many marks you will get for each element and how this fits into the overall marking scheme. Try your best to complete the full set of examples. This will help consolidate your learning and, if you are required to submit the worked examples, could contribute to your continuous assessment marks.

For discussion-based tutorials:

Work out your position with regard to the topic. Reflect on what you have read and begin to evolve your personal position or viewpoint on the topic. Gather together evidence that supports your viewpoint and note down key points.

Consider the question from different angles. With regard to assessment, in particular, consider your viewpoint critically and anticipate what the counter-arguments might be. Build up your response to the counter-argument. If you hold an opposing view, what would be the strengths and weaknesses of your argument?

GO And now . . .

20.1 Think about the make-up and behaviour of the tutorial groups in which you participate. There are many different ways in which your fellow students may approach tutorials, and you may need to adapt your own natural style of participation to suit. For example, if one person tends to hog the discussion, you might need to be more assertive than usual to make sure that you get a chance to demonstrate your engagement with the topic, and gain credit for this.

20.2 Relate your tutorial work to other forms of assessment. In the next tutorial you attend, think about the work done or the discussion that occurs and consider how this might be useful to you in terms of exam revision. Write up notes after the event or annotate any handouts you received with the conclusions you have drawn from the exercises or discussion.

▶

20.3 Learn from other forms of meeting. Tutorials are meetings and it will help you to develop your participation style if you look at the way that other meetings you attend are conducted. You might feel that a greater or lesser degree of formality makes the dynamic work better, for example. Learn from the tactics of others by watching their processes and strategies for putting their points across.

21 Assessments of practical and laboratory work

How to improve your marks

The marks awarded to practical assessments can make up a relatively large proportion of the total for a module. Gaining better grades requires preparation before hand, focussed effort during the practical or practical exam, and care with writing up or answering.

Key topic:

→ Forms of practical assessment and how to approach them

Key terms
Continuous assessment   Summative assessment

Practical work is generally included in the syllabus to complement the theory covered in lectures and tutorials. Depending on your discipline, it gives you a chance to see specimens, develop skills and understand how research is conducted. However, it is worth noting that, in some courses, the theory may not have been covered at the time of the practical, so it is advisable to do a bit of background reading prior to the practical class.

The importance that lecturers attach to practical elements of the course can be seen from the proportion of your overall module grade that they assign to these aspects. This may be between 30 and 50 per cent, so you should devote a proportionate amount of study and revision time to related assessment activities.

> ### Minimum attendance requirements
>
> In some courses, you must attend all or most of the practical classes. Failure to meet this minimum may mean you will not be given permission to sit the degree examination at the end of the year.

Consult your course handbook at an early stage to see how your practical work will be assessed. The main methods, including tips for tackling each one, are listed below.

Continuous assessment of lab work

This is a common way of assessing practical work, where grades are awarded for workbooks or lab reports completed during the course. As these marks may be relatively straightforward to achieve, this is a good way of building up a 'bank' of good grades so that it is easier to pass or do well in the overall module assessment. To maximise your marks for completed lab workbooks, ensure that your work in the lab is neat and tidy and you have completed all that is required of you.

Because lab work often seems rushed, neither of these aims may be straightforward to achieve, but both will be easier if you have prepared well. During lab sessions, check with demonstrators and staff that each part is completed to their satisfaction and take heed of their tips and suggestions.

When preparing a formal report from a practical, adopt the format laid out in your handbook or the lab schedule (which may differ among subjects). As marks are likely to be awarded for presentation, pay special attention to layout, print quality and order of sections. You may need to learn from lecturers' feedback how you can best approach writing style and the amount of detail required.

Practical exams

These 'summative' tests generally take place in laboratories during the main exam period. They usually involve:

- recall and understanding regarding specimens and techniques;
- tests of the observational and manual skills you have developed during the course;
- following procedures and using equipment;
- measurement and numerical analysis;
- interpretation or presentation of data.

Because of the 'unseen' and unpredictable nature of practical exams, there is less chance to prepare using standard revision techniques. You will need to be ready to think on your feet, adopting a logical approach. Make sure you read each question carefully (more than once) so you can carry out *exactly* what is required.

Examples of practical exam questions

The following are examples of typical question styles (imagine the precise context yourself):

Draw a fully labelled diagram of specimen A.

Graph the following data and draw conclusions.

Examine specimen N and photograph M; and describe how the specimen relates to this environment.

Construct a calibration curve for a . . . test using the reagents and/or equipment provided. What value do you estimate for the unknown specimen X?

Comment on the syndrome evident in slide B.

Prepare a pure sample of . . . using the reagents and equipment provided.

Examine Table Z (or picture A) and answer the following questions . . .

Given the data in Table F, calculate . . .

Compare specimens A and B, explaining . . .

Past papers for practical exams are rarely available, and if they are, may make little sense in the absence of the real samples. To help your revising, you could look through the past practical schedules, highlighting parts that might be amenable to this form of examination. Some examples of types of practical questions in the sciences are provided above. Spot tests and oral forms of practical exam may involve moving around a 'circuit', examining specimens, or perhaps looking at slides through a microscope, then providing quick written answers or responding with spoken answers. Key tips for this type of exam are:

- Always take your time when answering.

- Always take a second look at the specimen to check whether your first assumptions are correct.

- Start with simple points, such as a straightforward description of the specimen (the markers may be using a checklist with some marks attached to these basic points).

- Consider all aspects of the question.
- If you don't know an answer, don't waffle – move on to the next question quickly, if this is allowed.

Although you may think of the lab as an informal setting, formal practical exams will be subject to the same rules and regulations as written 'theory' exams. Some practical exams may be 'open book', where you are allowed to consult past schedules, for example, as you tackle the questions. However, don't assume this is the case unless you have been specifically informed.

Practical questions within written/online assessments

Sometimes you will find that practical elements are assessed as a component of exams that you might assume would be solely about theory. For example, there may be questions in multiple-choice and short-answer papers that relate to work done in practicals. Look at the 'small print' in your course handbook to see if this might be the case, or ask lecturers, and adjust your revision accordingly. For example, this might imply that you rehearse simple calculations and learn relevant formulae.

Don't think of practical work in isolation

You may be able to use information gained from practicals in essay-style answers, perhaps to provide relevant examples.

Practical tips for practical exams

Scan your practical schedules as an aid to revision. Try to see if you can predict possible question types, but avoid question-spotting. Memorise key procedures that might be tested, but bear in mind that there may be a limited time for each question on the paper. Think about the skills you may be asked to use and go through the instructions and tips you have been given about these.

Practise answering numerical questions. As recommended in Ch 18, this is the best way to ensure you perform well on the day if problem-solving is included in your practical exam.

Practise labelling diagrams. If you can identify a need to provide labels on diagrams of seen and unseen specimens, you may wish to test yourself by drawing up a schematic diagram, then labelling it without reference to supporting texts or schedules. This will give you feedback on how much you already know and what you need to learn (**Ch 12**).

Take advantage of 'open doors' revision sessions. In some subjects, the lab may be opened in the period prior to exams so you can have another look at key specimens. These sessions provide an opportunity to review the material and possibly ask questions of staff in attendance – very useful if you are unsure about some aspects, or think your memory will improve if you see the samples again, closer to the exam. These sessions are also an opportunity for collaboration with fellow students, as you can ask each other questions about the specimens to test your knowledge.

State the obvious, justify your conclusions. If you find that your mind has gone blank during a practical exam, start with the basics. For example, if asked to identify a specimen, do not give up because you can't immediately do this from memory. The question-setter may be trying to see if you can adopt a logical approach to the problem, and everyone in the class may be in the same situation. Start from first principles and basic observations ('the specimen has a yellow colour, therefore I conclude . . .') and move on from there. Similarly, when you do know an answer, state why you know it. There may be marks allocated to this aspect, which you will miss out on if you simply provide a bare answer.

Review good practice in graphing and tabulating. If constructing and interpreting data in graphs and tables might be a part of your exam, it makes sense to go over the basic principles and instructions for these forms of presentation beforehand.

Ensure that you have the correct equipment required for a practical exam. This will depend on the subject, but will be similar to the items taken to each practical. Remember to include a watch so that you can monitor time. Synchronise your watch with the clock in the exam hall so that you are working within the same time frame as invigilators and examiners.

And now . . .

21.1 Consult your course handbook. Find out what proportion of marks are allocated to practical assessment and what form the assessment will take. Adjust your revision plans accordingly.

21.2 Make a list of possible questions that might come up in your practical exam. This revision exercise might best be carried out working with a fellow student so that you can share ideas. Use the learning outcomes and schedules as a source of ideas.

21.3 Make up a checklist of equipment to take to the exam. It will boost your confidence to know that you have everything you might need ready beforehand, rather than grabbing things at the last moment.

References and further reading

Biggs, J., 1999. *Teaching for Quality Learning at University*. Buckingham: Society for Research into Higher Education and Open University Press.

Bloom, B. S., Englehart, M. D., Furst, E. J., Hill, W. H. and Krathwohl, D. R., 1956. *Taxonomy of Educational Objectives: Cognitive Domain*. New York: McKay.

Fleming, N. D., 2001. *Teaching and Learning Styles: VARK Strategies*. Christchurch: Neil D. Fleming.

Gardner, H., 1983. *Frames of Mind*. New York: Basic Books.

Gardner, H., 1993. *Multiple Intelligences: The Theory in Practice*. New York: Basic Books.

Graham, B., 2006. *The Role of Minerals and Vitamins in Mental Health*. Available at http://www.nutritional-healing.com.au/. Last accessed 16/1/07.

Holmes, T. H. and Rahe, R. H., 1967. 'The social readjustment rating scale', *Journal of Psychometric Research*, 11, 213-18.

Honey, P. and Mumford, A., 1982. *Manual of Learning Styles*. London: Peter Honey.

Honey, P. and Mumford, A., 1995. *Using Your Learning Styles*. London: Peter Honey.

Jones, A. M., Reed, R. and Weyers, J. D. B., 2003. *Practical Skills in Biology*, 3rd edn. London: Pearson Education.

Luft, J. and Ingham, H., 1955. 'The Johari window, a graphic model of interpersonal awareness', *Proceedings of the Western Training Laboratory in Group Development*. Los Angeles: University of California, LA.

Magistretti, P. J., Pellerin, L. and Martin J.-L., 2000. 'Brain energy metabolism: an integrated cellular perspective,' *Psychopharmacology: The Fourth Generation of Progress*. American Society of Neuropsychopharmocology. Available at http://www.acnp.org/Default.aspx?Page=4thGenerationChapters. Last accessed 14/05/07.

McKenna, P., 2006. *Make a New You with Paul McKenna: Sleep*. Available at http://www.timesonline.co.uk/article/0,,32769-2540709,00.html. Last accessed 16/1/07.

Myers-Briggs, I., 1995. *Gifts Differing: Understanding Personality Types*. Palo-Alto, California: Davies-Black Publishers.

Ritter, R. M., 2005. *New Hart's Rules: The Handbook of Style for Writers and Editors*. Oxford: Oxford University Press.

Rutherford, D., 2002. *Vitamins: What Do They Do?* Available at http://www2.netdoctor.co.uk/health_advice/facts/vitamins_which.htm. Last accessed 16/1/07.

Glossary of key terms

Terms are defined as used in the higher education context; many will have other meanings elsewhere. A term in colour denotes a cross-reference within this list.

Abbreviations:

abbr. = abbreviation

gram. = grammatical term

Latin = a word or phrase expressed in the Latin language, but not 'adopted' into English

pl. = plural

sing. = singular

vb = verb

Acronym (gram.) An abbreviation formed from the first letter of words to form a word in itself, e.g. radar, NATO.

Active learning Knowledge and understanding gained from doing an activity focussed on the module content, which involves thinking allied to some physical action, such as distilling notes and drawing mind maps.

Aggregate mark Sum of all the marks for a given course. Some elements may be given different weightings (i.e. count for more or less) than others.

Annotate To expand on given notes or text, e.g. to write extra notes on a printout of a PowerPoint presentation or a photocopied section of a book.

Assessment criteria The factors that will be taken into account in assigning a grade. See also Marking criteria.

Autonomous learner A student who has adopted strategies for undertaking personal responsibility for learning by organising study time, and assignment and other work schedules, as well as cultivating skills in critical thinking.

Brainstorm An intensive search for ideas, often carried out and recorded in a free-form or diagrammatic way.

Caffeine A stimulant alkaloid drug found in tea, coffee, many soft and energy drinks, and in 'keep-awake' tablets. Can disturb sleep patterns if taken late in the day and has diuretic properties.

Chronological Arranged sequentially, in order of time.

Chunking Breaking a topic down into more manageable bits.

Class exam The exam at the end of each term or module. Traditionally, class exams were formative in nature. See Formative assessment.

Continuous assessment Assessment throughout the academic year. Also known as in-course assessment.

Counselling Service provided by the institution to support students, giving guidance or advice, especially at times of personal stress or difficulty.

Critical thinking The examination of facts, concepts and ideas in an objective manner. The ability to evaluate opinion and information systematically, clearly and with purpose.

Dimensional analysis An analysis of a formula or equation where the units are substituted for the symbols: in theory, both sides of the formula should be equivalent in units.

Displacement activity An activity that takes the place of another, higher-priority one; e.g. tidying your room instead of studying.

Distilling To extract the important points. In note-making, focussing on the main points, headings and examples, minimising detail.

Distractor An incorrect option in a multiple-choice question. Ideally, distractors should not be easily identified unless the respondent knows the topic well.

Exam diet A block of exams; the period when exams are held.

Existentialist Sensitive to deep issues about human existence. In particular, believing in the freedom and responsibility of the individual.

External examiner An examiner from outside the institution whose role is to ensure that standards of examination are maintained.

Extrovert A person whose focus is on the external rather than themselves. Generally, a person who is outgoing, sociable and unreserved.

Finals The summative exams at the end of degree or a year. See Summative assessment.

Flash cards Used as a memory aid, these cards have a cue word/date/formula on one side and a meaning/significant event or development/proof on the other side. Students may opt to use these as a tool in revision.

Formative assessment An assessment or exercise with the primary aim of providing feedback on performance, not just from the grade given, but also from comments provided by the examiner. Strictly, a formative assessment does not count towards a module or degree grade, although some marks are often allocated as an inducement to perform well. See Summative assessment.

Instruction words The words indicating what should be done; in an exam question or instruction, the verbs and associated words that define what the examiner expects of the person answering.

Introvert A person whose focus is on the internal self rather than the external. Generally, a person who is shy, withdrawn and reserved.

Invigilator A person who supervises an exam and ensures that university regulations are followed during the exam.

Johari window Developed by Joe Luft and Harry Ingham, and called after the first letters of their names, the Johari window method looks at pairs of contrasting aspects of an issue or situation and organises information or viewpoints within a two-by-two grid. The original Johari technique was designed to aid self-assessment of personality, but the grid technique can be used for other contexts.

Kinesthetic Regarding learning personality, someone who learns best from physical activity, by using their senses, or by recalling events in which they were involved.

Law of diminishing returns A principle that states that there is a point in a process when little is gained for extra effort put in. In the context of exams, the point beyond which few marks will result from continuing with a particular answer and where applying effort to other questions might be more productive.

Learning objective What students should be able to accomplish having participated in a course or one of its elements, such as a lecture, and having carried out any other activities, such as further reading, that are specified. Often closely related to what students should be able to demonstrate under examination.

Learning outcome Similar to a learning objective, often focussing on some product that a student should be able to demonstrate, possibly under examination.

Learning style The way an individual takes in information, processes it, remembers it and expresses it.

Marking criteria A set of 'descriptors' that explain the qualities of answers falling within the differing grade bands used in assessment; used by markers to assign grades, especially where there may be more than one marker, and to allow students to see what level of answer is required to attain specific grades.

Marking scheme An indication of the marks allocated to different components of an assessment, sometimes with the rationale explained.

MBTI (abbr.) Myers-Briggs Type Inventory: a categorisation of personalities.

Micronutrients Also known as trace elements, are dietary elements (cf *vitamins*) required in small quantities that are essential for efficient metabolism and physiological function.

Mnemonic An aid to memory involving a sequence of letters or associations, e.g. 'Richard of York goes battling in vain', to remember the colours of the rainbow: red, orange, yellow, green, blue, indigo, violet.

Mock exam A practice exam, e.g. using a past exam paper and conducted with similar timing to the real exam.

Model answer An example answer provided by a tutor or examiner to an exam question, or potential exam question, sometimes indicating where marks will be allocated and why.

Multiple-choice question (MCQ) A type of question where several possible answers are given and the candidate must identify the correct answer.

Multiple intelligence Subdivision of intelligence into various categories more or less pronounced in different people, which influence the way they process information.

Negative marking A form of marking used especially in multiple-choice questions where a mark or marks are deducted for giving an incorrect answer. This acts to reduce any incentive to guess answers.

Nightline A charitable organisation run by students of London universities, providing emotional support for students and an information service (www.nightline.niss.ac.uk).

Numeracy The ability to use numbers, understand mathematical concepts and carry out standard mathematical operations.

Oral exam An exam carried out by discussion with the examiner(s).

Part-marking A type of assessment, where marks are awarded to the component parts of an answer. This often includes allocating marks for adopting the correct process to arrive at an answer and for the presentation of the working and answer, and not solely for stating the correct answer at the end.

Peer assessment An assessment where grading, or part of it, is provided by fellow students.

Perfectionism The personal quality of wanting to produce the best possible product or outcome, sometimes regardless of other factors involved.

Personal pronoun (gram.) Word referring to people. Can be first person (e.g. I), second person (e.g. she) or third person (e.g. they); subjective, objective and possessive. Additionally, applicable to words such as 'ship', which are referred to as 'she'.

Practical A laboratory-based course component. Sometimes also used to refer to a field visit.

Prioritising Ranking tasks in precedence, taking into account their urgency and importance.

Quantitative Data (information) that can be expressed in numbers, e.g. the width of the lecturer's tie or the number of elderly patients included in a survey.

Question-spotting Guessing which specific topics will be asked about in an exam, and how the questions will be phrased.

Revision timetable A schedule for study that subdivides the time available among the topics that need to be revised.

Rote learning Learning by memorising, where knowledge is acquired but not necessarily with comprehension.

Rubric In the context of exams, the wording at the top of the exam paper, concerning timing, numbers of types of questions that must be answered, and candidate details that must be supplied on the answer paper.

Samaritans A charitable organisation providing emotional support for people who are experiencing feelings of distress or despair, including those that may lead to suicide (www.samaritans.org.uk).

Short-answer question (SAQ) A type of question where only a few sentences and paragraphs are required in answer, or perhaps the drawing or labelling of a diagram.

Stress A response to some form of external pressure, resulting in mental or emotional strain or suspense, typified by worrying, fretting and agonising.

Study buddy A mutual arrangement between two or more students studying the same or similar subjects, who agree to support each other in their learning by conducting joint study sessions.

Summative assessment An exam or course assessment exercise that counts towards the final module or degree mark. Generally, no formal feedback is provided. See Formative assessment.

SWOT analysis This is a framework that presents a style of analytical assessment. The student lists aspects of the situation under scrutiny in the context of four headings - Strengths, Weaknesses, Opportunities and Threats.

Transcript The certified details of a student's academic record, e.g. modules taken, performance in exams and modules, as recorded by a university.

Tutorial A small-group meeting to discuss an academic topic.

Value judgement A statement that reflects the views and values of the speaker or writer rather than the objective reality of what is being assessed or considered.

Vitamins Organic dietary compounds (cf micronutrients) required in small quantities, that are essential for efficient metabolism and physiological functioning.

Writer's block The inability to structure thoughts; in particular, the inability to start the act of writing when his is required.